MW01148194

COLLECTED WRITINGS OF CHAIRMAN MAO

VOLUME 1

POLITICS AND TACTICS

By

Mao Zedong

El Paso Norte Press
Special Edition Books

Collected Writings of Chairman Mao – Volume 1
Politics and Tactics

By Mao Zedong

Edited by Shawn Conners
Translation by Foreign Language Press, Peking

First Edition – November 2009

Published by
EL Paso Norte Press
El Paso, Texas USA

ISBN10 1-934255-25-4
ISBN13 978-1-934255-25-4

Printed in the United States of America

CONTENTS

Collected Writings of Chairman Mao: Politics and Tactics

Mao Zedong

COLLECTED WRITINGS
OF
CHAIRMAN MAO

POLITICS AND TACTICS

PART 1

BASIC TACTICS

Mao Zedong

CHAPTER I
INTRODUCTORY REMARKS

HOW THE POPULAR MASSES CARRY OUT MILITARY ACTION

How is it that the bare-handed masses, banded together in ill-armed military units without guns or bullets, are able to charge the enemy, kill the enemy, and resolutely carry out effective action in the war? This is a very widespread and very reasonable query. But if we know the function of the weapons used by an army and the aim of an army's action, we can then understand how our popular masses, although bare-handed, still have weapons and can engage in action to subdue the enemy.

The principal function of an army's weapons is simply to kill the enemy, and an army's final aim is simply to reduce or destroy the enemy's fighting strength. Well, in our daily life, is there any object that cannot be used to kill the enemy or any type of action that cannot reduce or destroy his fighting strength? For example, a kitchen knife, a wooden cudgel, an axe, a hoe, a wooden stool, or a stone can all be used to kill people. Such actions as cutting electric lines, destroying bridges, starting rumors, spreading poison, or cutting off supplies can everywhere inconvenience the enemy or reduce his fighting strength. All these are methods we may be unwilling to utilize or unable to employ. If we really want to kill and exterminate the enemy, there are weapons for us everywhere and work for us to be doing at all times, in order to ensure effective united action by the army and the people.

POINTS OF SPECIAL ATTENTION

After from this, we must pay special attention to the present war on the national level, which has become cruel beyond our imagination and has also lasted a long time. We must not, because we are undergoing the suffering of a war more cruel than any seen in the past, immediately capitulate; nor must we, under the influence of a long war, suddenly lose our endurance and give way to lassitude. We must inspire ourselves with the most resolute spirit of unyielding struggle, with the most burning patriotic sentiments, and with the will to endurance, and carry out a protracted struggle against the enemy. We must know that, although the circumstances and the duration of the war are cruel and protracted, this is nothing compared to what would happen if the war were lost; if our country were destroyed and the whole of our people reduced to a position of irretrievable ruin, the suffering would be even more cruel and would never come to an end. Therefore, however cruel the war may be, we must absolutely and firmly endure until the last five minutes of struggle. This is especially the case with our present enemy, who finds his advantage in a rapid decision in the war, whereas our advantage is to be found in the strategy of a protracted war.

WE MUST NOT FEAR THE ENEMY

When we see the enemy, simply because he has a weapon in his hands, we must not be frightened to death like a rat who sees a cat. We must not be afraid of approaching him or infiltrating into his midst in order to carry out sabotage. We are men; our enemies are also men; we are all men, so what should we fear? The fact that he has weapons? We can find a way to seize his weapons. All we are afraid of is getting killed by the enemy. But when we undergo the oppression of the enemy to such a point as this, how can anyone still fear death? And if we do not fear death, then what is there to fear about the enemy? So when we see the enemy, whether he is many or few, we must act as though he is bread that can satisfy our hunger, and immediately swallow him.

DEFINITION OF GUERRILLA WARFARE

When it is not advantageous for our main land army to meet the enemy in large-scale engagements and we, therefore, 'send' out commando units or guerrilla units, which employ the tactics of avoiding strength and striking at weakness, of flitting about and having no fixed position, and of subduing the enemy according to circumstances, and when we do not oppose the enemy according to the ordinary rules of tactics, this is called employing guerrilla tactics.

CHAPTER II
TACTICS

At a time when our country's national defense preparation are not completed, and when our weapons are inferior to the excellent equipment with which the enemy has provided himself, we must observe the following principles whenever we wish to wage a battle with the enemy:

PRECAUTIONS WHEN ON THE MARCH

When we are on the march, we must send plainclothes units armed with pistols ahead of our vanguard, behind our rear guard, and to the side of our lateral defenses, in order to spy out the situation and to forestall unexpected attacks by the enemy, or superfluous clashes.

PRECAUTIONS DURING HALTS

When we encamp, if there is a presumption that the enemy may be near, we should send every day a guerrilla company—or at least a platoon—toward the enemy's defenses to carry out reconnaissance at a distance (from 20 to 30 *li*) or to join up with the local forces and carry out propaganda among the masses, in order to inspire them to resist the enemy. If this unit discovers the enemy, it should, on the one hand, resist him and, on the other hand, report to us so that we can prepare to meet the foe or to retreat without being drawn into an unnecessary battle.

WE MUST NOT ATTACK STRONG POSITIONS

If the enemy guards his position firmly or defends a strong strategic point, then, unless we have special guarantees of success, we must *not* attack him. If we attack him, we will waste considerable time, and our losses in killed and wounded will certainly be many times those of the enemy. Moreover, in guerrilla warfare, our artillery is not strong: if we recklessly attack a strong position, it will be very difficult to take it rapidly, at one stroke, and, meanwhile, it will be easy for the enemy to gather his forces from all sides and surround us. On this point, the army and the people must be absolutely firm of purpose and cannot act recklessly in a disorderly fashion because of a moment's anger.

DO NOT FIGHT HARD BATTLES

If we do not have a 100 per cent guarantee of victory, we should not fight a battle, for it is not worthwhile to kill 1,000 of the enemy and lose 800 killed among ourselves. Especially in guerrilla warfare such as we are waging, it is difficult to replace men, horses, and ammunition; if we fight a battle and lose many men, and horses, and much ammunition, this must be considered a defeat for us.

WE MUST NOT FIGHT IF THE SITUATION OF THE ENEMY IS NOT CLEAR

When we are encamped in a certain place and suddenly discover the enemy but are not informed regarding his numbers or where he is coming from, we must absolutely not fight, but must resolutely retreat several tens of *li*. It is only if we are right up against the enemy that we should send covering units, for, if the enemy comes to attack us, it is certainly because his forces are superior or he has a plan, and we must under no circumstances fall into his trap. If the enemy is in force, it is obviously advantageous to retreat. If his numbers are small and we retreat, nothing more than a little extra fatigue is involved, and there will always be time to return and attack him again later.

WE MUST ORGANIZE THE MASSES AND UNITE WITH THEM

Modern warfare is not a matter in which armies alone can determine victory or defeat. Especially in guerrilla combat, we must rely on the force of the popular masses, for it is only thus that we can have a guarantee of success. The support of the masses offers us great advantages as regards transport, assistance to wounded, intelligence, disruption of the enemy's position, etc. At the same time, the enemy can be put into an isolated position, thus further increasing our advantages. If, by misfortune, we are defeated, it will also be possible to escape or to find concealment. Consequently, we must not lightly give battle in places where the masses are not organized and linked to us.

USING THE MASSES TO MAKE A SURPRISE ATTACK AND BREAK A BLOCKADE

When the enemy surrounds us and blockades us, we should rouse the popular masses and cut the enemy's communications in all directions, so that he does not know that our army is already near him. Then, we should take advantage of a dark night or of the light of dawn to attack and disperse him.

SURPRISE ATTACKS ON ISOLATED UNITS

When we have reconnoitered the enemy's position and have kept our men at a distance of several *li* and when he has unquestionably relaxed his precautions, then we advance rapidly with light equipment, before dawn when the enemy does not expect us, and exterminate him.

USING THE POPULAR MASSES TO HARRY THE ENEMY

On the basis of a decision by the main force of the army, in time of battle, we send out part of our forces, divided into several units—the smallest element being a platoon—to lead the local militia, police, volunteer army, or other popular masses of the peasantry and the workers. These groups use a great variety of flags, occupy mountaintops or villages and market towns, use brass gongs, spears, rudimentary cannon, swords and spikes, trumpets, etc. They scatter all over the landscape and yell, thus distracting the enemy's eyes and ears. Or, both night and day, on all sides, they shoot off isolated shots to cause panic among the enemy soldiers and fatigue their spirit. Then, afterward, our army appears in full strength when the enemy does not expect it and disperses him by a flank attack.

CIRCLING AROUND TO GET AWAY FROM THE ENEMY

When we are faced with a large enemy force and do not have sufficient strength to meet its attack, we use the method of circling around. We hasten to a place where there are no enemy troops, and we use mountain trails so that the enemy cannot catch up with us. At the same time, along the way, we utilize the popular masses, getting them to carry on reconnaissance work in the front and the rear, so that we are not attacked, by the enemy from either direction.

GETTING OUT OF DIFFICULT SITUATIONS

Presume that in the rear there is a pursuing army and in the front an obstacle, or that the pursuing army is too strong for us. As a plan to get out of such a difficult situation, we can send a part of our forces 4 or 5 *li* off, to lure the enemy up a big road, while our main force follows a side road and escapes the enemy. Or we can make a detour around to the enemy's rear and attack him there by surprise. Or we can use the local militia and the police to go along another route, leaving some objects, making footprints in the road, sticking up notices etc., so as to induce the enemy to follow them. Then, our main force suddenly rushes out from a side road, striking at the enemy from the front and the rear, encircles him on all sides, and annihilates him.

CAUSE AN UPROAR IN THE EAST, STRIKE IN THE WEST

When the army wants to attack a certain place, it does not advance there directly but makes a detour by some other place and then changes its course in the midst of its march, in order to attack and disperse the enemy. "The thunderclap leaves no time to cover one's ears."

CONCEALED ATTACKS FROM AMBUSH

When the enemy is pursuing us in great haste we select a spot for an ambush and wait until he arrives. Thus, we can capture the enemy all at one stroke.

AMBUSHING THE ENEMY IN THE COURSE OF HIS MARCH

When we learn from reconnaissance that the enemy plans to advance from a certain point, we choose a spot where his path is narrow and passes through confusing mountainous terrain and send a part of our troops—or a group of sharpshooters— to lie hidden on the mountains bordering his path, or in the forest, to wait until his main force is passing through. Then we throw rocks down on his men from the mountains and rake them with bullets, or shoot from ambush at their commanding officers mounted on horseback.

MAKING A STRONG DEFENSE BY EMPTYING THE COUNTRYSIDE

When our spies have informed us that the enemy is about to arrive, and if our force is not sufficient to give battle, we should then carry out the stratagem of "making a strong defense by emptying the countryside." We hide the food, stores, fuel, grain, pots and other utensils, etc., in order to cut off the enemy's food supply. Moreover, as regards the popular masses of the area in question, with the exception of old men, women, and children, who are left behind to provide reconnaissance information, we lead all able-bodied men to hiding places. Thus, the enemy has no one to serve as porters, guides, and scouts. At the same time, we send a few men to the enemy's rear communication lines, to cut off his supplies, capture his couriers, and cut or sabot age his communications facilities.

MEETING A SUPERIOR ENEMY

1. When the enemy advances, we retreat. If the enemy's forces were weaker than ours, he would not dare advance and attack us. So, when he advances toward us, we can conclude that the enemy is certainly coming with superior force and is acting according to plan and with preparation. It is, therefore, appropriate for us to evade his vanguard, by withdrawing beforehand. If we meet with the enemy in the course of our march and either do not have clear information regarding him or know that his army is stronger than ours, we should, without the slightest hesitation, carry out a precautionary withdrawal.

As to the place to which we should withdraw, it is not appropriate to go long distances the main roads, so that the enemy follows us to the end. We should move about sinuously in the nearby area, winding around in circles. If the enemy appears ahead of us, we should circle around to his rear, if the enemy is on the mountains, we should descend into the valleys; if the enemy is in the middle, we should retreat on the two sides; if the enemy in on the left bank of the river, we should retreat on the right bank ; if the enemy is on the right bank, we should retreat on the left bank.

Moreover, in withdrawing, when we come to a crossroads, we can deliberately leave some objects in the branch of the road we do not take or send a small fraction of our men horses that way, in order to leave some tracks or write symbols. Or we can write some distinguishing marks on the road we do take to indicate that it is closed. Thus, we induce the enemy to direct his pursuit and attack in the wrong direction.

At such times, it is best to evacuate the popular masses and such armed forces as the militia, police, volunteer army, etc., by various routes in all directions, in order to confuse the enemy's eyes and ears. We can leave behind part of our men, who bury their uniforms and weapons and disguise themselves as merchants, street vendors, etc. They spread rumors or pretend to be obliging in order to spy out information regarding the enemy's numbers, his plans, the location and routine of his camps, and the precautions he is taking. If the enemy questions them about the direction in which we have withdrawn and the strength of our force, they should talk incoherently, pointing to the east and saying the west, pointing to the south and saying the north, replacing big by small and small by big, talking at random and creating rumors. They wait until our army is about to attack, and then they dig up their uniforms and put them on, take out their weapons, and attack the enemy from his midst, thus completely routing him and leaving him with nowhere to turn.

2. When the enemy retreats, we pursue. When the enemy army retreats, it is appropriate to take advantage of the situation to advance. On such an occasion, the enemy's military situation must have undergone a change, otherwise he would not have retreated, and he is certainly not prepared to join battle against us with any resolution. If we take advantage of the situation and make a covering attack on his rear, the enemy's covering units will certainly not be resolved to fight, and in the context of the enemy's over-all plan it will be difficult for his forward units to return and join in the fray. In rough mountainous terrain, where the paths are narrow and rivers and streams intertwined so that there are many bridges, even if the enemy's forward forces were to turn back, this move would require much time. So, by the time he turns back, his rear will already have been annihilated and he will already have been disarmed.

At this time, the organizations of the popular masses, should devise methods for destroying the bridges on the route over which the enemy is retreating, or cutting the wires of his communications system. Or, best of all, they should wait until the bulk of the enemy's army have retreated and, taking advantage of the protection afforded by our guards and army, block the enemy's path of retreat, so that, although his forces may want to turn back, they cannot do it, and, although they yearn for help, they cannot obtain it.

But, at such a time, the most important task of the popular masses is to spy out the direction in which the enemy is withdrawing, in order to ascertain whether or not there may be an ambush or a feigned retreat intended to encircle us from two sides, and report to us immediately so that our army can pluck up courage and pursue the enemy or devise a method of evading him.

3. When the enemy halts, we harass him. When the enemy is newly arrived in our territory, is not familiar with the terrain, does not understand the local dialect, and is unable to gain any information from the scouts he send out, it is as though he had entered a distant and inaccessible land. At such a time, we should increase our harassment—shooting off guns everywhere, to make him ill at ease day and night, so exercising a great influence on both his mind and body under such circumstances, I fear that any army, however overbearing, will begin to waver and will become weary. We need only await the time when his spirits are wavering and his body weary, and then, if our armies rush in all together, we can certainly exterminate him completely.

DEALING WITH A WEAK ENEMY

Fighting as we are for the existence of our nation and the achievement of the aims of guerrilla warfare—which are to destroy the enemy and to stir up the courage of the popular masses— when we are faced with a weak enemy, naturally we should unite with the popular masses of the place in question to surround him and exterminate him at one stroke.

AROUSING THE MASSES

There are always a good many among the popular masses who forget the great cause for the sake of petty advantage. Frequently having received great favors from the enemy, they act contrary to conscience and aid the forces of evil. For this reason, before the arrival of the enemy in a given place, we must do our utmost to whip up the spirits of the popular masses, to rouse their will to resist and to endow them with an unshakable resolve to fight to the end, without seeking advantage, without compromise or surrender. We must induce them to follow our orders sincerely and to cooperate with our army to resist the enemy. At the same time, we should also organize "resist-the-enemy associations", "associations for national salvation", and other types of professional bodies to facilitate the transmission of orders and the evacuation of villages in time of necessity and to clean out traitors and prevent their utilization by the enemy.

CHAPTER III
THE AIM OF THE WAR

The ultimate aim of guerrilla warfare is certainly to disarm the enemy, to destroy his fighting strength, to get back the territories he has occupied and to save our brethren whom he is trampling under foot! But when, because of objective circumstances and other factors of various kinds, it is impossible to attain this goal, it sometimes happens that the areas unaffected by the fighting are controlled by the enemy in all tranquility. This should not be. Because of this possibility, we must think up methods for inflicting economic and political damage in these areas and destroying communication facilities, so that, although the enemy has occupied our territory, it is of no use to him and he decides to withdraw on his own initiative.

In guerrilla warfare, we must observe the principle "To gain territory is no cause for joy, and to lose territory is no cause for sorrow." To lose territory or cities is of no importance. The important thing is to think up methods for destroying the enemy. If the enemy's effective strength is undiminished, even if we take cities, we will be unable to hold them. Conversely, when our own forces are insufficient, if we give up the cities, we still have hope of regaining them. It is altogether improper to defend cities to the utmost, for this merely leads to sacrificing our own effective strength.

CHAPTER IV
ORGANIZATION

OPPORTUNITIES FOR ORGANIZATION

1. When we are devoting ourselves to warfare in an open region, it is the sparsely populated areas, with a low cultural level, where communications are difficult and facilities for transmitting correspondence are inadequate, that are advantageous.

2. Narrow mountainous regions, rising and falling terrain, or areas in the vicinity of narrow roads—all of which are inconvenient for the movement of large bodies of troops— are also advantageous.

Opportunities also exist:

3. When the people in the enemy's rear are in sympathy with our army.

4. When the enemy is well-armed, and his troops numerous and courageous, so that we have to evade direct clashes.

5. When the enemy has penetrated deeply into our territory and we are preparing everywhere to carry out measures of harassment and obstruction against him.

6. Dense forests or reedy marshes, in the depths of which we can disappear, are most advantageous for this purpose, especially in the late summer and autumn, when we find ourselves behind a curtain of green.

FORMS OF ORGANIZATION

The action of a guerrilla unit takes one of the following forms:

1. We send out a large cavalry unit from our main force, together with mounted artillery, or cavalry accompanied by a platoon or more armed with light automatic weapons. They penetrate as rapidly as possible into the enemy's rear destroy there all his communications links, and carry out the thorough and complete destruction of all his storehouses of food, grain for his horses, and ammunition. Moreover, they send out a small group of their forces to destroy all places of military significance in the enemy's rear. Once these forays have been carried out, the group fights its way out in another direction and rejoins the main force.

2. We send out cavalry or a special task group of infantry. Their strength should be from a platoon to a few companies. They should penetrate as deeply as possible into the enemy's rear and, moving rapidly and unpredictably, should carry the battle from one place to another. When there is no alternative, or when the enemy is not expected to arrive before a certain time, they can also dwell temporarily in secret where they are. As required by the exigencies of the situation, they can employ either all or a part of their forces. They return when the time comes that they can no longer stay in the enemy's rear, or when the task entrusted to them is completed, or because the enemy has already discovered our traces and our intentions, and has taken effective measures of defense.

3. In the enemy's rear, we choose some young, strong, and courageous elements among the local population and organize some small groups who will accept the leadership of the experienced and trained persons we send out or of experienced persons whom we had trained previously in the place in

question. The secret activity of these small groups involves moving from their own area to another one, changing their uniforms, unit numbers, and external appearance, and using every method so as to cover their tracks to the utmost.

4. Or we seek volunteers from our army and provide them with high-quality light weapons, in order to form them into special guerrilla units under the leadership of such officers as have benefited from experience and study.

5. Guerrilla units can be classified according to their nature. Those formed of selected volunteers are called special guerrilla units. Those organized generally from a part of our army are called basic guerrilla units. Those organized from the local population are called local guerrilla units. When basic and local guerrilla units engage in combined actions, they are subject to the unified command of the commander of the basic unit.

6. As for the choice of the members of a guerrilla unit, the members of a basic guerrilla unit should be taken from among those soldiers who are healthy, firm of purpose, patient, courageous, and quick-witted. Moreover, the soldiers themselves be willing to join the group in question. In the case of the independent actions carried out by these men in the course of guerrilla operations, there is generally no way to verify whether or not their tasks are executed in accordance with orders, and frequently they act beyond the knowledge of the responsible commander. For this reason, the choice and training of members of guerrilla units should have as its central theme "faithfully carrying out one's task."

7. The choice and the nomination of the commander of a guerrilla task group or small group requires even greater forethought and reflection. The capacity of the commanders for faithful and courageous action, their military knowledge-

especially their knowledge of guerrilla tactics-their possession of a lively intelligence and the ability to adapt rapidly to changing circumstances, their loyalty, and their daring are indispensable conditions for carrying out plans and completing our tasks.

NUMBER OF TROOPS

The number of men belonging to a guerrilla unit is determined by the tasks, but it commonly ranges from five or ten men to something over a thousand. However, the maximum strength of such a unit may not exceed one regiment. If the number of soldiers is too large, the movements of our forces will be encumbered, there will be greater difficulties regarding food supply, and it will be difficult to conceal the troops by the use of false uniforms. Because of these problems, our plans may be discovered or revealed before they have been carried out. Moreover, replenishing our supplies of ammunition will be a problem. Furthermore, we will often have difficulties because of poor roads, with the result that not only will all our plans prove merely illusory, but also we will often fall into difficulties to no good purpose in going and returning.

The great superiority of a small guerrilla unit lies in its remarkable mobility. With very little expenditure of time and effort, one can get food, and it is also easy to find a place to rest, for one does not need much in the way of rations or a place of shelter to camp. Still less is one held up by bad roads, and supplies of ammunition and medicine are also easy to replenish. If we do not succeed in our operation, we can retreat in good order.

TYPES OF SOLDIERS

As for the type of soldiers employed in guerrilla units, cavalry, engineers, and highly mobile infantry troops are excellent. Cavalry is entrusted with the task of creating disorder on the enemy's flanks, and also, when we are pursuing the enemy, with that of maintaining pressure on his rear guard and creating confusion on his flanks and in his rear. Moreover, at all times, cavalry is the guerrilla unit's only instrument for transmitting correspondence and for reconnoitering. Hence, the cavalry is indispensable to any guerrilla unit. Engineers are used for destroying communications in the enemy's rear (such as railroads, telephone and telegraph lines, bridges, etc.) As for the highly mobile infantry units, they are useful to startle the enemy and produce in him a feeling of insecurity night and day.

WEAPONS

Apart from the rifles of the infantry and the cavalry, light machine guns, hand grenades, etc., guerrilla units should also be supplied with pistols and submachine guns.

To the extent that the terrain permits it, one can also add heavy machine guns, mortars, and small cannons.

MEN AND BAGGAGE

Convenience of movement and agility being the characteristics of a guerrilla unit, the baggage train, cases of equipment and ammunition, etc., should all be kept as simple as possible for the sake of convenience. The combatant and noncombatant members of the unit should all be organized as most appropriate for guerrilla warfare, and all other persons who are not indispensable should be kept to the strict minimum.

1. The officers and men in each guerrilla squad should not exceed 8; each platoon should not exceed 26; and each company should not exceed 100.

2. When automatic weapons are somewhat more numerous, the number of men can be still further reduced, and guerrilla units composed of 5 or 6 men can be sent out repeatedly, in order to achieve the greatest results in terms of harassing the enemy or securing intelligence.

3. Each commanding officer of a unit should have only one orderly at most. Apart from this according to the complexity of the tasks, two or three officers should share the services of one orderly. Even more attention should be accorded to not abusing this rule by unnecessarily increasing the number of couriers as a substitute for orderlies and to seeing that an unnecessarily large number of men are not sent to carry out a given task, thereby reducing the fighting strength of one's own unit. Hence, when one sends out couriers, one must reflect carefully on whether they can accomplish their task or not.

4. It is preferable that each mass unit should not carry bundles of food. When the dry rations carried separately by each soldier are exhausted, one should take advantage of opportunities to borrow the pots and pans of the population so as to prepare supplementary rations. If it is necessary to carry bundles, each unit should not carry more than two.

5. Bundles of writing materials should not be carried in excess of needs. Normally, two bundles per regiment, one per battalion, and one per company are permissible. The weight of each bundle should not exceed 40 kilograms.

6. Each officer and soldier should carry his own bedding, knapsack, etc. Bearers should not be engaged to transport these items. This rule should be firmly established in advance.

OBJECTS TO BE CARRIED

A guerrilla unit preferably should have the following things:

1. Equipment and explosives for destroying railroads, telephone and telegraph lines, arsenals, etc.

2. Medicines. Those needed in case of emergencies should be carried according to the season, but dressings, etc., should be provided on a permanent basis.

3. A compass, and maps of the area in which the guerrilla unit operates.

4. Light radio equipment, which is especially important in order to be able to report at all times on the situation of the enemy and to listen in on the enemy's reports.

5. A certain quantity of gold coins, to provide for unexpected needs and for buying food.

DISCIPLINE

Whether or not the military discipline of a guerrilla unit is good influences the reputation of our whole army and its ability to secure the sympathy and support of the popular masses. Only strict discipline can assure the complete victory of all our independent actions. Consequently, our attitude toward those persons who violate military discipline, harm the people's interest, and do not resolutely execute the orders of their superiors, should consist in punishing them severely without the slightest regard for politeness. The application of military discipline in a partisan unit does not aim exclusively at punishment. Rather, it aims at strengthening the political instruction of the officers and men and raising their level of political consciousness, thereby indirectly eliminating a large number of actions contrary to military discipline and causing the officers and soldiers to understand the psychology of the masses, so that at appropriate times they can unite effectively with the common people.

POLITICAL ORGANIZATION

1. Each guerrilla task group and small group should have a political director, and in the headquarters of the guerrilla unit there should be a political training department, for directing the political work of officers and soldiers and dealing with the human problems of all the political instructors.

2. Each mess unit of a guerrilla unit should establish a special commissioner in order to guard against the infiltration and activity of reactionary elements and to encourage those soldiers without clear ideological consciousness who are wavering in their purposes.

3. In order to prevent desertion by the soldiers, a committee against desertion, as well as "groups of ten," should be organized in each guerrilla unit. The groups of ten and the committee against desertion are negative methods for preventing desertion. Their organization and work should be carried out roughly as follows:

    a. In order to prevent desertion, every guerrilla unit should establish a desertion committee and every mess unit should organize a group of ten.

b. The committee against desertion should be composed of from seven to nine people, one of them being the chairman and the others members. It should be composed of lower-level cadres who can endure difficulties and whose thinking is friary, as well as heads of the groups of ten. The groups of ten are composed of ten men in all, one of them being the head and the others members. They are made up of faithful and reliable soldiers.

c. The over-all activity of the groups of ten is subordinated to the committee against desertion. As regards military matters, it is subordinated to the commander of the unit and to the committee against desertion. In other work, it is subordinated to the political training department. Both groups of ten and committees against desertion must accept the guidance of their commanding officer.

d. The work of the group of ten should take account of all the actions and talk of the officers and soldiers, especially of "camp idlers" and such. Unstable elements should be secretly watched, even if they are members of the group of ten or their friends.

e. Meetings should be held once a week to review the work and to report to the commanding officer and the committee against desertion regarding the situation in general at all times. After each extreme difficulty or when our army has suffered a slight defeat and is staying in its base camp, special attention should be paid to unfavorable attitudes that may develop among the soldiers and to conversations that may endanger the morale of the soldiers.

f. The work of the committee against desertion consists above all in reviewing the work of the groups of ten and in admonishing and guiding them at the appropriate times. The committee may also call conferences of the heads of all the groups of ten, or plenary conferences of all the members of the groups, to discuss the progress of the work as a whole.

g. The soldiers' life is rather like living in the desert, and every day the men undergo the fatigue of political study and training in the art of combat. This may easily engender feelings of disgust and opposition. In order to provide entertainment for the army and to compensate for a dull life, one should establish in a guerrilla unit clubs or amusement rooms.

SPECIAL FORMS OF MILITARY ORGANIZATION

1. In order to make up for insufficient supplies of ammunition and poor marksmanship, every company should have: from three to nine sharpshooters, to be employed exclusively for shooting from ambush at long distances or for shooting at special targets (enemy officers, machine-gunners or artillery-men, couriers, etc.) .

2. The commander of each task group and small group should choose particularly sharp-eyed couriers to serve as observes. Normally, a task group commander should have two of these, and a small group commander one. These men serve exclusively to remedy the insufficiency of battlefield observation.

3. Each task group and small group of a guerrilla unit should have two nurses, who devote themselves exclusively to emergency care of sick officers and soldiers and to instruction in hygiene.

4. In order to obtain reliable information regarding the enemy's disposition, so as to be able to oppose him without losing any opportunities, all guerrilla units should establish groups of

scouts. Normally, it will be sufficient if each unit has one platoon, each task group has one squad, and each small group a smaller element. A network of local scouts should also be established by the group of scouts wherever they go, or by scouts concealed in advance.

CHAPTER V
TASKS

The principal object of the action of a guerrilla unit lies in dealing the enemy the strongest possible blows to his morale, and in creating disorder and agitation in his rear, in drawing off his principal force to the flanks or to the rear, in stopping or slowing down his operations, and ultimately in dissipating his fighting strength so that the enemy's units are crushed one by one and he is precipitated into a situation where, even by rapid and deceptive actions, he can neither advance nor retreat.

1. Destroy railroads and highways within the area of action, as well as important structures along the roads. Telephone lines and telegraph systems are especially important.

2. Destroy the enemy's principal or secondary supply depots.

3. Destroy the enemy's storehouses of food and military equipment.

4. Strike in the enemy's rear, at his baggage train, or at his mounted and unmounted couriers, as well as at his mounted scouts, etc. Also seize the provisions and ammunition that the enemy is bringing up from the rear to the front.

5. Strike at the enemy's independent task groups and at the inhabited areas that he has not yet solidly occupied.

6. Mobilize and organize the popular masses everywhere and aid them in their own self-defense.

7. Destroy airfields and military depots of the air force in the enemy's rear.

CHAPTER VI
OPERATIONS

ACTION

1. The first principle lies in careful and secret preparation, and in rapid and sudden attack. Fierce wind and heavy rain offer a favorable occasion for a guerrilla attack, as do thick fog, the darkness of night, or circumstances in which it is possible to strike at an exhausted enemy.

2. The operations of a guerrilla unit should consist in offensive warfare. Whether its numbers be great or small, such a unit can nonetheless appear where it is not expected and, in its attacks, take advantage of the enemy's lack of preparation. But when there are indications that the situation is unfavorable, or when there is no certainty of victory, it is appropriate to withdraw rapidly, so as not to suffer damaging losses. If the attack originally planned by the guerrilla unit fails to give an advantageous result, and, the enemy goes over to the offensive, a guerrilla unit should withdraw quickly. Only when the enemy pursues us, and it is impossible to evade his attacks, can we fight a defensive action and then gradually withdraw.

THE USE OF TACTICS

1. The redoubtable force of a guerrilla unit definitely does not depend exclusively on its own numerical strength, but on its use of sudden attacks and ambushes, so as to "cause an uproar in the east and strike in the west," appearing now here and now there, using false banners and making empty demonstrations, propagating rumors about one's own strength, etc., in order to shatter the enemy's morale and create in him a boundless terror. In addition, we must pay attention to such principles as: "The

enemy advances, we retreat, the enemy retreats, we advance, the enemy halts, we harass him," camouflaged attacks, etc.

2. A really excellent stratagem for bringing the enemy to his destruction lies in mobilizing the popular masses, in making a strong defense by emptying the countryside, in luring the enemy to penetrate our lines deeply, in cutting his communications, in placing him in a position where he has difficulties with his food supply, where his men are weary and the terrain is unfavorable and then launching an attack.

3. By such tactics as sudden attacks, ambushes, making a strong defense by emptying the countryside, etc., a guerrilla unit should make every effort to avoid positional warfare, and all frontal engagements. Before the local guerrilla units have received regular military training, they should not be launched against the enemy in a regular and prolonged battle. For this reason, when local guerrilla units are first formed, they should be used only in conjunction with actions by basic or special guerrilla units. It is only after a certain period that they can act independently.

4. If we strike at the point where the enemy feels the greatest difficulties, in order to draw his main force to come to the relief of the position, then, afterward, we send our main force somewhere else, either to attack other isolated and weak forces of the enemy or to attack his reinforcements on the march.

ADVANTAGEOUS AND DISADVANTAGEOUS TERRAIN

1. Because open terrain affords very little good cover, it is slightly disadvantageous for us when guerrilla units operate there. Covered, mountainous, or broken terrain are all advantageous for us.

2. A guerrilla unit should be thoroughly familiar with the terrain in its region of action and should think frequently about the ways in which it can appear from a place where the enemy army does not expect it, following secret and hidden routes such as valleys, forests, or narrow winding paths, so as to approach close to the enemy army and take advantage of a situation in which the enemy, persuaded he is quite secure, has taken no measure of defense whatsoever. Then, following the principle that the "thunderclap leaves no time to cover one's ears," the unit can strike sudden blows and then vanish into hiding without a trace, thus reducing the enemy to a level where he does not feel secure whether he is withdrawing or advancing, attacking or defending, moving or remaining still, sitting or lying down.

3. Relatively large villages, market towns, and places where there is a reasonably large amount of grain and other moveable property are frequently the objects of enemy attack and harassment. A guerrilla unit should regularly spy out the enemy's traces, and prepare an ambush so as to attack him when he is in the midst of his march.

4. A guerrilla unit should use every method, within its area of action, to prevent the enemy's small units from entering. and his main force from concealing itself there. In case of necessity, a guerrilla unit should also strive to unmask the military strength, disposition, and plans of the enemy operating outside its area of action.

SEASONS

A guerrilla unit must consider the seasons (winter, summer, or autumn are suitable for operations), with reference to the strength of our forces and those of the enemy, and especially with reference to the weapons of war; it must also be thoroughly familiar with the organization of the enemy's rear. Whether or not each season is favorable to us is also determined with reference to the terrain.

SECRET ACTION

The peculiar quality of the operations of a guerrilla unit lies entirely in taking the enemy by surprise. Consequently, we must take every possible measure to preserve military secrecy, as described in detail below:

1. The commander of the unit should explain to his subordinates their tasks and the plan for the operation only just before the action begins, or while they are advancing. In case of necessity, he should explain the whole plan only by stages, so that others learn about each stage only when required.

2. The best method for the transmission of orders in a guerrilla unit is by oral explanations from the commander to his subordinates. It is necessary to limit written orders insofar as possible, in order to avoid leakage of military secrets.

3. One should not discuss the whole of one's actions and plans with guides or the local population. This is the case even with regard to local populations favorable to us; it is even more necessary to forbid such talk when we are about to attack a certain place.

4. We should send out faithful and reliable scouts in advance to observe the point where we are going to camp or to lie in ambush along important roads in the enemy's rear, in order to cut off his information.

5. When we advance, our rear guard should take full responsibility for obliterating and removing all secret signals

and road signs. We should also advance by circuitous route, so that the enemy does not know the direction of our advance.

6. Fixed code names should be used in place of all unit designations, and the use of the real names of units should be strictly prohibited.

7. Except in case of necessity, all documents should be burned immediately after they have been read.

8. Apart from the methods already enumerated, the true plans of a guerrilla unit can also be obscured in certain cases by using the local population for the deliberate propagation of false information about the operations of the guerrilla unit, in order to deceive the enemy.

ARRANGEMENTS AND PREPARATIONS FOR MOVEMENT

In order that our movements may be rapid, apart from doing our utmost to simplify all our organization, we should at all times maintain excellent preparations for action (investigation and intelligence regarding the front, care of sick soldiers, preparation for guides, preferably employing local peasants whose sympathies lie with the guerrillas, or other reliable persons), and we should also preferably carry three days' dry rations. If this is done, then when we want to move, we move, and when we want to stop, we stop, and there is no need for special arrangements.

THE CONDITIONS FOR VICTORY

1. A condition for the victory of a guerrilla unit is that the officers and soldiers have an absolutely courageous and resolute spirit. They must also be filled with a spirit of action in

common, and be thoroughly alert and resolved to carry out their own tasks. Apart from this, they must have healthy bodies and be able to endure boundless hardships, be good at the use of their weapons, etc.

2. A guerrilla unit should not lose heart in difficult times, nor should it cease its activity if it encounters difficult circumstances. As regards their confidence in ultimate victory, their confidence in the success of their cause, and especially their hatred of our national enemy, such circumstances should only strengthen their purpose to advance courageously in spite of all obstacles.

UNITED ACTIONS

If a small guerrilla unit, because its numbers are insufficient, cannot carry out a task assigned to it, it can unite temporarily with a few other guerrilla units, in order to fulfill its task.

Guerrilla operations are best carried out under cover of night.

CHAPTER VII
SURPRISE ATTACKS

POINTS THAT SHOULD BE CAREFULLY CONSIDERED
REGARDING OUR TASKS BEFORE A SURPRISE
ATTACK

When a guerrilla unit has finished concentrating for an attack, and when plans for scouts, courier service etc., have all been satisfactorily completed, and one is preparing a surprise attack on a certain inhabited place, the commander of the guerrilla unit must first form a clear idea about each of the following points.

1. What is the strength of the military forces defending the given inhabited place? How are they deployed? How are they armed? What is their fighting capacity? How many scouts to sound a warning have they sent out?

2. Is there any other enemy nearby? If there is, how far away is he? Can he quickly come to the aid of the defending forces? Can we imagine how he would come to aid them? From what direction he would come?

3. What sort of roads are there that could be followed by the guerrillas and by the enemy? What hidden roads are there in the vicinity of the place we intend to attack by surprise? What route will we take to get to the place we are attacking? The preceding three points are not only things we should know in view of carrying out a surprise attack; we must also not fail to consider them with reference to our withdrawal after the attack.

4. As for fixing the time of a surprise attack, it is best to carry it out at night, for, under the cover of darkness, even if the attack should fail, it can still inspire panic in the enemy. But we can

attack at night only if we are thoroughly familiar with the terrain, and have clearly understood the enemy's dispositions or have extremely good guides. Otherwise, we should choose instead to carry out such surprise attacks at daybreak. If a surprise attack is to be directed against a supply depot, it should be carried out in the dead of night, for the men, horses, and military equipment in such a depot will be on the move again very early, at daybreak.

5. Can the population of the given inhabited place aid the enemy or not? How can we prevent the population from bringing trouble on itself in this way?

While we should think through our plans at length, we should avoid overly subtle plans.

POINTS FOR ATTENTION BEFORE SETTING OUT

1. Before setting out, a guerrilla unit should complete all its preparations for the march (see below). Moreover, it should consider taking stretchers for transporting wounded soldiers.

2. The method for a surprise attack on the enemy should be thoroughly understood beforehand not only by the commander of the unit and the commanders of each task group, but also by all the members of each independent task group. The best mode of transmitting this information is through oral explanations by the commander and his staff. Written orders of all kinds should be held to a minimum, in order to avoid having their contents divulged by loss or mistake.

3. Prior to setting out, all officers at every level should appoint a replacement, in order, on the one hand to express their resolution to sacrifice themselves and, on the other hand, to avoid the risk that, if they are wounded or killed, the action of

the guerrilla unit may fail to attain its objective because of them, thus influencing the whole situation.

POINTS FOR ATTENTION WHILE ON THE MOVE

1. We must make the greatest efforts to conceal the movements of a guerrilla unit and to prevent discovery by the enemy. Consequently, while advancing, we must leave the highroads and avoid large villages, and choose out-of-the-way places or even places where there are no roads at all, advancing along narrow winding trails. But we should keep away from miry roads, so as to avoid excessive fatigue.

2. When advancing, we should not proceed for long time on the same road, for this makes it easy for the enemy to discover our tracks. From the standpoint of keeping our movements secret, it is also generally appropriate to move by night, even when we are advancing a long distance.

3. When we are advancing, for the sake of concealing ourselves, we should hold the number of people we send out for reconnaissance to the very lowest level. In general, it will be sufficient to send just a few scouts along the road, but we must have very good guides.

4. If we are not absolutely certain that there are no enemy spies coming to observe us, it is best to divide our forces into small groups, which advance separately in different directions and then concentrate at a point which has been secretly designated.

5. When a guerrilla unit is on the move, it should be constantly prepared for a meeting with the enemy. For this reason, the commanding officer of a guerrilla unit generally advances, accompanied by his staff, just behind the scouts, behind the elite soldiers, or ahead of the staff of the unit (the staff is

entrusted to the leadership of the second in command). Thus, it is easy to obtain a clear picture of the situation, and decisions can be taken very rapidly. If the commander sees that it is possible to advance, he advances; if he becomes aware of difficulties, he withdraws. All that is required is for two or three officers to hold a discussion, and then the decision can be made. Thus, we avoid sending orders back and forth, with the consequent wasting of opportunities, and we diminish command form the rear, and its attendant evil of taking action not in keeping with the circumstances.

6. Apart from the scouts sent out along the road, the soldiers of the guerrilla unit should not load their rifles, so as to avoid accidental discharges during the march and discovery by the enemy.

MEASURES TO BE TAKEN IF THE ENEMY IS ENCOUNTERED WHILE ON THE MARCH

1. Under no circumstances should a guerrilla unit provoke a pointless battle before it has reached its objective. Even though a guerrilla unit may encounter the enemy in the course of its march, it should devise a way for getting around him—if necessary, departing from the original plan. If there is no way of avoiding battle, we should emerge from ambush, after rapid preparations, so as to appear where the enemy does not expect us and annihilate him by a surprise attack. At the same time, when we are carrying out such a maneuver, we should pay attention to whether the enemy halts or advances, and send out scouts to reconnoiter from all directions. If the enemy army is not prepared for battle or if, although he is in some strength, he is not on the alert, we should charge him immediately. Otherwise, we should remain in hiding and quietly await an opportunity.

2. When, in the course of our march, we encounter enemy outposts or scouts, we should avoid being seen by them and circle past them in strict silence. But it we encounter a situation in which we judge there is an opportunity to be grasped, we should act rapidly and capture them without firing a shot.

DISPOSITION OF TROOPS DURING A SURPRISE ATTACK

When a guerrilla unit carries out a surprise attack, the disposition of its troops should be more or less as follows:

1. We should launch a fierce attack by our main force on the point in the enemy's disposition where it hurts the most — a really swift and resolute sudden blow. We should also send another force around to carry out energetic action on the enemy's flanks and in his rear, in order to confuse his judgment, and prevent him from fathoming where our main force is located.

2. We should attack one point in the enemy's disposition with all our might, but we should also carry out feigned deployments in other places and make an empty demonstration with a few scattered soldiers, so as to confuse the enemy's eyes and ears, and disperse his forces.

3. If we can determine beforehand the enemy's line of retreat, then we should, within the limits of what is possible, send a part of our forces to intercept him. Ii the enemy has his heavy artillery and logistic supply installed outside the village, then we should designate a special small group to seize them.

4. If the guerrilla unit is numerically strong, it should be divided into several columns and should carry out the attack from two, three, or several directions, attempting to cut off the

enemy's retreat, But we should consider the matter thoroughly, so as to avoid causing confusion in our own ranks, which might result in erroneously taking our own troops for those of the enemy. Because of this possibility, it is necessary, in advance of the action, to agree on signals.

5. In the case of a surprise attack on the enemy, if there is reason to fear that enemy reinforcements may arrive from a certain direction, we should send a small body of troops in advance of the action to the route where the reinforcements may arrive, so as to obstruct their advance, or report this peril to the main force.

6. At the time of a surprise attack, the choice of the point on which the brunt of the attack will fall, and the geographical distribution of our forces (in general, two-thirds of our men are used for the principal direction of attack, and only one-third for the auxiliary directions of attack) must absolutely be such as to prevent the enemy forces from spreading out or receiving reinforcements and to make it possible for us to smash them one by one.

7. The various task groups making up a guerrilla unit should divide their forces within a very short distance of the point where the attack is to be made, and from there make a separate but coordinated advance. The best place for this is the point from which the charge will be made. In this way, we can avoid such misfortunes as losing our way, or the premature division of our forces, and we can also guard against the danger of surprise attacks by the enemy. For the farther apart are the various independent columns or groups, the more likely they are to be separated by the terrain, and the more difficult it will be to expect them all to strike at the same moment.

THE SUCCESS OF A SURPRISE ATTACK

In general, we charge the enemy when he is not prepared, in circumstances where he is frightened and flustered. If we really want to strike when the enemy is not expecting us and attain success, the following points should be attended to:

1. We must act rapidly and secretly and not allow our plans to be revealed prematurely.

2. We must strike at a time when the enemy's warning system is not very alert.

3. We must make an empty display, and attack in several places at once, so that the enemy's reaction is confused, his forces are frightened and hamper one another, and he cannot use all his strength to resist us stubbornly.

4. In carrying out the surprise attack, we must attack at the appointed hours; there must be no noise; no shots must be fired; there must be no battle cries. We must make every soldier understand the use of the arms employed in a surprise attack, which are the bayonet and the hand grenade. We must not return fire simply because we hear the gunfire of the enemy. It is only when we have an opportunity to take advantage of the situation to attack the enemy that we should launch our attack, with our vanguard well supported by our rear guard, choosing frontal, flanking, or direct blows.

DISPOSITIONS FOLLOWING THE SUCCESS OF A SURPRISE ATTACK

1. As soon as the tasks of a surprise attack have been carried out, a guerrilla unit should rapidly withdraw. Before withdrawing, it is best to go a few *li* in a false direction, and

then afterward turn and go in our true direction, so that the enemy will be unable to discover our tracks, and will not be able to follow us.

2. It is not appropriate for a guerrilla unit to take along prisoners, or to acquire large amounts of booty, which hinder our movement. It is best to require the prisoners first to hand over their weapons, and then to disperse them or to execute them. As for booty, it should be dispatched by the local government, or by the population.

3. During the battle, three officers and men out of every company should be given the exclusive task of picking up and gathering together abandoned rifles and ammunition. After a victorious battle, we should devote all our efforts to collecting everything on the battlefield, and we can also call upon the population of nearby areas to gather such things together, so that not the smallest trifle is left behind.

DISPOSITIONS FOLLOWING THE DEFEAT OF A
SURPRISE ATTACK

If a surprise attack is defeated, we should rapidly withdraw to the place of assembly designated in advance. The usual assembly point is in the place where we encamped the previous night. If our forces are sufficient, we can leave a reserve unit along the designated withdrawal route, to look out for prisoners and wounded men.

CHAPTER VIII
ESPIONAGE

POINTS FOR ATTENTION WHEN CARRYING OUT ESPIONAGE

1. All reports on the situation should be transmitted without loss of time to one's superiors or to friendly armies.

2. The reports which we collect absolutely must be in full detail. All sloppy and negligent reporting must be severely prohibited.

3. The scope of espionage is not limited merely to the situation of the enemy; spies should also pay attention to the terrain. We should be informed of all aspects of the terrain that are disadvantageous to us, especially those aspects favorable to the enemy, such as narrow roads, river crossings, circuitous routes for avoiding these river crossings and narrow roads, etc.

4. We should bend every effort to obtain complete and detailed information regarding all matters having any relation to our guerrilla unit; our efforts should never cease until we understand the situation thoroughly.

5. We should pay attention to the sentiments of the people toward ourselves and the enemy. Are the people actively aiding us? How is their positive attitude manifested?

METHODS OF ESPIONAGE

Apart from sending out courageous and intelligent individuals (i.e., spies) to carry out espionage on every hand, a guerrilla unit must unite closely with the popular masses of the place in question. Moreover, in strategically important places, we use reliable local inhabitants or those among the people who sympathize with the guerrilla unit (for example, we can make use of feudal relationships and find a relative, or someone belonging to the family of person who has been executed by the enemy; we can also employ those among the people who hate the enemy, etc.). We give these people a relatively good salary, establish a secret espionage network, as well as a system of sentries, so that we can transmit information with facility.

ESPIONAGE REGARDING THE NUMBER OF THE ENEMY'S TROOPS, HIS TACTICAL SKILL, AND HIS ARMAMENT

1. Where are so and so many enemy infantrymen, cavalrymen, artillery-men, and other units to be found? How many armored cars and trains, tanks and air planes does the enemy have? And where are they?

2. What kind of defensive works does the enemy have in his front, in his rear, and around his cities and other places? What kind of forces are defending?

3. Where are the enemy's encampments and arsenals?

4. What about the enemy's reserves and flanking troops? Where are they?

5. How is the morale of the enemy soldiers? Are they prepared to fight or not? What are their relations with the people and with their own officers?

6. What about the enemy army's supplies of military equipment, bedding and clothes, food, and other items?

ESPIONAGE REGARDING THE TERRAIN

1. First of all, we must pay attention to the important roads within this area, as well as their direction, their width, their type of surface, whether or not they are muddy, etc., and whether or not they are suitable for use by all types of forces.

2. Are there any forests or not? If there are, we must pay attention to the kinds of trees, and to their area.

3. We must consider rivers, their width and depth, their rate of flow, the slope and type of soil of the banks. Are there bridges, ferries, or other means for crossing the river? If there are bridges, will they bear up under artillery, the baggage train, and other types of unit?

4. Are there any marshes? Where? What is their area? Can they be crossed or not? If so, we must note what kinds of troops can get through them.

CHAPTER IX
AMBUSHES

TYPES OF AMBUSH

When we emerge suddenly from hiding, and strike a sudden blow at the enemy who is just passing by, this is called an ambush. The sole habitual tactic of a guerrilla unit is the ambush. By means of an ambush it is extremely easy to obtain a good result, and as a general rule they are always advantageous. Such action is divided into the following types:

1. Ambush by luring the enemy. This occurs when our troops, so to speak, prostrate themselves and hold out both arms, enticing the enemy to penetrate deeply. It is carried out by first placing our main force in ambush along the two sides of the road, or in a hiding place on one side, and then attacking the enemy with a small force. This force then feigns defeat and withdraws, luring the enemy deep into our lines, after which the main force rushes out from one side or both sides and carries out a surprise attack.

2. Waiting ambushes. These are very similar to ambushes by luring the enemy, but it is not necessary for a part of our forces to feign defeat. Instead, we establish an observation post on some height, to observe the movements of the enemy army, and when his main force has reached the appropriate point, we rush out and attack him by surprise.

SPOTS FOR CARRYING OUT AMBUSHES, AND OBJECTIVES TO BE ATTACKED

Ambushes can be carried out against a variety of objectives such as isolated enemy soldiers, couriers, whole mobile units, logistic convoys, transport columns, trains, etc. Further details are given below.

1. When ambushing the enemy's cavalry or infantry, we should choose a spot where they cannot use their weapons and where it is not easy for them to manifest their full strength.

2. Ambushes against logistic convoys or transport columns should be carried out in the midst of a forest or in the countryside.

3. Ambushes of small enemy units, or whole mobile units or motorized transport columns are most valuable. But we must first understand their plans, the direction in which they are advancing, and the time it will take them to pass. We must also reflect in detail on the location for the ambush and carefully seek out a place likely to contribute to a favorable result. At the same time, we must carefully select in advance the route for our own withdrawal.

4. When a guerrilla unit carries out an ambush against a railroad train, our forces can be split into three parts. The first part should take up battle positions near the railroad, to guard against resistance from the train. The second part should take up a position on the two sides of the train, and shoot into the carriage. The third part has the task of charging and boarding the train to make a search, unloading the cargo, taking charge of the weapons, etc.

THE TERRAIN IN AMBUSHES

The point at which an ambush is carried out must have the following features:

1. It must have good cover, in order to prevent our being observed by the enemy and, at the same time, permit us to observe the enemy.

2. It must permit us to employ our maximum fire power.

3. It must allow us to leap out rapidly at one bound from ambush and come to grips with the enemy. Hence, between the point where we lay in ambush and the enemy, there should be a dense forest, a damp depression, a narrow road, or some other intervening ground.

THE DISTANCE FROM WHICH AN AMBUSH SHOULD BE CARRIED OUT

If the guerrilla unit which carries out a surprise attack is in sufficient strength so that it wants to come to grips with the enemy at one bound, then it should stage its ambush near the side of the road. If, on the other hand, the enemy is in considerable strength, and our plan is merely to harass him and cause confusion, then we should remain in a place some distance from the road.

IMPORTANT TRICKS FOR AN AMBUSH

1. An ambush can most advantageously be carried out in silence. Whether by day or night, loud talking should be absolutely forbidden, as should patrolling along the front.

2. Remaining a long time in ambush can easily lead to discovery of our plans and an increase in the danger. Because of remaining too long in ambush, the state of tension of our men is gradually weakened, and they can no longer maintain their vigilance. Hence, one can easily be discovered by the enemy. A point that especially merits attention is that, if we

have already been discovered by the enemy, we should immediately either launch our attack or withdraw.

CHAPTER X
SURPRISE ATTACKS ON THE ENEMY'S FORAGING UNITS

OCCASIONS FOR SURPRISE ATTACKS

A charge against the enemy's foraging units should be carried out under the following circumstances:

1. It can be executed when the enemy unit is nearing a village.

2. We can wait until the enemy enters a village and has scattered in all directions to forage from door to door, and then carry it out.

3. We can wait until the enemy has finished foraging and is returning loaded with booty, and then attack by surprise from ambush.

4. Which of the above types of attack is most appropriate should be determined with reference to the circumstances, by the persons who are responsible for the guerrilla unit. They should carefully evaluate all the factors and make arrangements adapted to circumstances.

SURPRISE ATTACKS IN A VILLAGE

It is most advantageous to attack the enemy's foraging units in a village. At such a time the greater part of the enemy's foraging unit is scattered all over the place, and it is not easy for them to gather together quickly. But, in carrying out this type of surprise attack we must steal by the enemy's warning outposts or capture his sentinels without the slightest sound; only then can we make our attack.

SURPRISE ATTACKS OUTSIDE A VILLAGE

It the force carrying out a surprise attack is especially weak, it must wait until the foraging is completed and until the foraging column has reached a place favorable to a surprise attack—such as when it is passing through a forest, across a bridge, or along a narrow road—before attacking.

THE OBJECTIVES OF THE SURPRISE ATTACK

When a guerrilla unit has attacked and dispersed the enemy unit covering a foraging operation, it can reckon only that it has completed part of its attack. It must also destroy or capture all of their wagons. Consequently, the guerrilla unit should first engage the enemy covering unit in combat and then attack the logistic convoy with its main force and capture it.

POINTS TO WHICH THE GUERRILLA UNIT SHOULD PAY ATTENTION

It is easy to obtain the assistance of the local population when attacking one of the enemy's foraging units. Hence, within the limits of what is possible, part of the property seized should be given to the popular masses, to heighten their courage.

CHAPTER XI
SURPRISE ATTACKS ON THE ENEMY'S TRANSPORT UNITS

An attack on a transport column is one of the most advantageous forms of action for a guerrilla unit, since we can obtain in this manner the weapons, food, and supplies we need.

SUDDEN SURPRISE ATTACKS

With such attacks, we can frighten the enemy out of his wits, and precipitate him into a state of complete confusion. The coolies of the transport units are, in large part, timid peasants forcibly impressed. Moreover, the size of the covering force is limited, and it is generally spread out over a very long distance. If we overturn one of the wagons, we can make all the wagons behind it stop too.

METHODS OF ATTACK

1. The guerrilla unit must not forget that its task is not to defeat the enemy, but to capture the enemy's wagons. Consequently, we should detail only a part of our forces to do battle with the enemy's covering unit. The rest of our men should be ordered to plunder, pursue, and demolish the materials he is transporting. Hence, whenever we carry out such a surprise attack, we should do our best to contrive matters so as to open fire rapidly against the transport unit and cause them to stop, in order to increase their confusion and fear.

2. In order to stop the whole transport column, it is only necessary to shoot at the front part of it, because, under conditions of mass anxiety and bewilderment, when the wagons in front stop, they will interfere with one another, fall over on the side of the road, and bring about a situation of

extreme confusion. If there are a large number of transport wagons, and if, because the front of the column is under fire, the wagons at the rear endeavor to turn around and escape, the guerrilla unit should send out a small number of riflemen to shoot furiously from cover at the tail end of the column, so that it does not dare turn around.

3. If the unit carrying out the surprise attack is in an inferior position, and the covering unit is taking active precautionary measures, the guerrilla unit should exhaust the enemy by incessant false alarms, and then when the transport column is passing through a forest or valley or along a narrow road in some other type of terrain, where the enemy's logistic convoy cannot easily turn around, the attack should be swiftly carried out. It is not often advantageous to carry out a surprise attack on a baggage train in a village, for the covering unit and the logistic convoy can easily make use of the houses and other cover, and offer strong resistance.

4. If the covering unit has already been dispersed by our attack, the resistance of the transport unit has also been overcome, and enemy reinforcements cannot arrive in time, the guerrilla unit can then destroy the wagons and the goods they are carrying or destroy completely whatever the guerrillas cannot carry away or have no use for.

CHAPTER XII
THE CORRESPONDENCE NETWORK OF A GUERRILLA
UNIT AND THE DESTRUCTION OF COMMUNICATIONS
FACILITIES IN THE REAR

THE OBJECT OF THE NETWORK

So that they may be able to call upon one another for aid and
receive information at all times regarding the situation of the
enemy, guerrilla units should do their utmost to maintain the
closest and most solid relations with the local population for
the exchange of correspondence.

MEANS FOR MAINTAINING RELATIONS

In order to set up such a correspondence network, we should,
in addition to utilizing the telephone in the greatest possible
measure, employ all means at hand. These include runners,
messengers on horseback, messengers on bicycles, secret
couriers posted in advance for transmitting information, as well
as transmittal by sentries, and even signals and pre-established
signs, etc.

METHODS FOR TRANSMITTING REPORTS

1. A network for important correspondence should be set up.
Reports of an urgent character can best be transmitted by
messengers on horseback. When this is impossible, we should
send out reliable individuals particularly good at going on foot.
It is also possible to arrange in advance for the transmittal of
secret letters. There are times, too, when we must send out
several men, each of them taking a different route, to make
certain that the report in question will reach its destination.

2. As for ordinary reports that are not particularly important, they are commonly transmitted by runners or messengers on bicycles. There are times when one can also use faithful individuals from among the local population who are thoroughly familiar with the routes to carry such reports.

SIGNALS FOR COMMUNICATIONS

For the sake of convenience in guiding each guerrilla group or unit by day or by night, in its actions in mountainous terrain or in forests, the commander of a guerrilla unit should establish in advance a certain number of basic signals and signs.

DISPOSITIONS REGARDING ROUTES OF
COMMUNICATION IN THE REAR

Should we or should we not destroy the routes of communication in the enemy's rear? We must reflect in detail about this problem. If we conclude that, in the future, our own army will not need to utilize these roads, or will not be able to utilize them, then we can destroy them.

POINTS FOR ATTENTION IN DESTROYING ROUTES OF
COMMUNICATION

If we want to destroy routes of communication, we must be thoroughly familiar with the terrain. It is only then that, moving rapidly and elusively, we appear suddenly and quickly withdraw. In eliminating the enemy's sentries, we must not fire a shot, in order not to alert them and give them a chance to flee.

PRECAUTIONS WHEN BEGINNING THE DESTRUCTION OF ROUTES OF COMMUNICATION

When we begin the destruction of routes of communication, we must first send out a detachment to the place where the presence of the enemy has been reported, in order to keep an eye on the enemy's patrols and his small detachments, so that they cannot quickly and secretly get close to the point where our own unit is at work. If, while beginning work, we are discovered by the enemy, we should shoot at him to keep him from coming nearer.

METHODS OF DESTROYING WORKS ON THE GROUND

1. Railroads should be destroyed at the points where they are most difficult to repair, such as at curves, at points where the railway is hidden from view, where the enemy's precautions are lax, where we can work under cover, or where we can destroy a large length of track. When destroying the rails, we should bend them, or hollow out the ground beneath them. In low-laying places we should dig ditches. As for tunnels, we should obstruct them.

2. Railroad ties, wooden bridges, telegraph and telephone poles, etc., should be burned up. Wires should be carried away or dropped into the water.

3. Signals switches, semaphores, railroad carriages, etc., located in the stations should be destroyed, preferably by blowing them up with explosives.

4. In destroying cobblestone roads, highways, bridges, and other constructions, we must in all cases choose a method of destruction appropriate to the nature of the construction.

CHAPTER XIII
REGULAR HIDING PLACES AND PRECAUTIONS TO BE
TAKEN WHEN WE HALT

MARSHALING OUR TROOPS

The problem is not merely one of resting and marshaling out troops. We require a place that can also be used for conserving ammunition and food and for receiving and looking after wounded and sick soldiers. Hence, the place in question commonly serves also as a supporting point in time of battle. As soon as we are the objects of the enemy's pursuit and attack, we withdraw there, and secretly hide, so as to await an opportunity to act or to begin resisting the enemy again.

THE CHOICE OF A SPOT

1. A hiding place where we can rest for a long time may conveniently be found deep in the forest, in a thatched hut near a marsh, in a cave under the ground or in a mountainside, on a lonely farm, or in a small and secluded hamlet. Because of the sympathy it enjoys a small guerrilla unit normally has no difficulty at all in finding a regular hiding place.

2. A guerrilla unit must absolutely maintain the strictest secrecy regarding the hiding places it has selected. Even one's closest friends and relatives must not be informed if they have no connection with the guerrilla unit in question. If our original hiding place has been discovered by the enemy, then, in general, we should not wait for the enemy to come and attack us but must quickly remove elsewhere.

3. Sometimes such hiding places also serve as storehouses for military equipment, powder, and provisions, and also for receiving wounded and sick soldiers. More often, a separate

secret location in the vicinity of the hiding place is selected for each type of storehouse because there are people continually going in and out of a hiding place and it can very easily be discovered by the enemy.

4. The more individuals there are among the people who support the guerrillas, so that the guerrilla unit can also maintain a communications network among the people, the easier it is for the guerrilla unit to find a hiding place. There are times when, in order to evade the enemy's pursuit and attack, and find a good place to hide, a given guerrilla unit must be split up, each of its members being obliged to find a way to hide himself in one of the houses of the local population. In such circumstances, the local population is the only hope of salvation of the members of the guerrilla unit.

THE QUESTION OF PROVISIONS

In places where the local population is hostile to the guerrillas, there is no alternative to foraging backed by force, but one should send reliable people from among the detachment, in order to guard against pillaging.

When the guerrilla unit does not fear discovery, it can send out a special small unit to forage for food, to collect contributions of food, or to demand food supplies from the local authorities.

CHANGING ONE'S HALTING PLACE

The best method by which a guerrilla unit can maintain its own security is through the agility of its action. In case of necessity, the unit can make a habit of changing its halting place every night (if, during the day, it has been in village A, at twilight it moves to village B).

OCCUPYING A HALTING PLACE

When a guerrilla unit encamps, the arrangement of its forces should be determined entirely by the nature of its action, but it should not occupy a large village that its own forces are insufficient to hold. If a guerrilla unit cannot do otherwise, and finds itself in such a place, it should occupy only a few collective dwellings situated apart and convenient for defense. The best thing is to be located in a village where one can keep a lookout in all directions, especially on the road along which the enemy might come. We must absolutely not disperse the members of the unit to stay in different houses, acting, for the sake of individual convenience, in a way of which the enemy could take advantage. In order to keep the enemy from knowing where we are staying, the best method is to enter the village only late at night. Moreover, we should look about carefully and all sides of the village and not allow anyone at all to come out.

THE DEGREE OF PRECAUTIONS

In order to avoid excessive fatigue to the members of a guerrilla unit, and to assure them of a real rest, it is not necessary to send out large numbers of scouts to sound a warning. It suffices to arrange for military outposts and concealed scouts in all adjoining places and along all roads (those which the enemy must take, or those related to us). We should also send out spies to places from 2 to 4 *li* away. This distance will be sufficient.

Whether or not the enemy attacks us, we must always fix an assembly point at a distance of from 10 to 16 *li*, for use in case of withdrawal. Moreover, the roads leading to the assembly point should be designated and marked in advance (but there must be at least two roads giving access to such a place).

PREPARATIONS

When a guerrilla unit is staying in a place, all its members, whether they be officers or soldiers, must at all times take measures to prepare for battle. Especially after twilight, every officer and soldier must gather together the arms and other equipment he carries with him, and arrange them in proper order, so that it will be convenient, in case there is an alarm in the dark, for him to go out quickly and meet the attack.

WHEN THERE IS ANXIETY ABOUT A SURPRISE
ATTACK BY THE ENEMY

1. If the guerrilla unit itself is especially alert, if its intelligence network is organized with exceptional discretion, and if the people of the area are in sympathy with us, so that they regularly report all movements to us, then it is extremely difficult for the enemy to mount sudden surprise attacks. But whatever the circumstances may be, we must always exercise due caution.

2. In order to prevent the enemy relying on a hostile population from coming and making a surprise attack on us, we must take special precautionary measures. Thus by methods of intimidation we warn the local population, we arrest and detain people. But at the same time, the unit must exercise caution and be prepared.

3. If there is an alarm, we should assemble the whole unit in a building that has been prepared for defense. We should dispatch to this building advance sentries and observers as required. The entrance to the building should be closed by movable obstacles, and we should establish in advance signals for the defense. Weapons and other equipment should be properly prepared and placed within reach of each man.

4. When circumstances are extremely critical, part of a friendly unit should take over responsibility for the security of our position and the place in which our army is staying, as well as for sending out spies far and wide to add to the warning system. They report constantly to the guerrilla task group on the situation of nearby enemy forces.

5. When we use artificial obstacles to block the roads, we must make provision for communication with our first line and reserves, as well as with the local population and our correspondence network.

6. In case of necessity, the roads within villages can be completely blocked off, or we can leave a way through. Whenever possible, each guerrilla task group should have a prepared position.

DISPOSITIONS IN CASE OF AN ENEMY SURPRISE ATTACK

1. When we discover that the enemy is moving toward us, if we find out from reconnaissance that he is not in strength, we should annihilate him with one sudden blow. If the enemy forces are several times more numerous than ours, we should rapidly withdraw. But while we are withdrawing we should give the enemy a false impression of the direction in which we are moving, so as to conceal our actual route of withdrawal.

2. If the enemy attacks us by surprise and we do not succeed in evading him, we should exploit in full measure the advantages of a village for defensive action, resist him firmly, and then later take advantage of an opportunity to withdraw.

3. If we have already lost a village, we should reply by a counterattack or counterblows in order to take it back quickly

and save our captured comrades, or those comrades who are clinging to a position and defending it stubbornly to the death. If our action is rapid, we can always attain such objectives, because after a victory the enemy is often in great confusion and lax in his precautions.

4. The best occasion for carrying out such counterblows, or such a counteroffensive, is just after the victory of the enemy's surprise attack. The sacrifices of a charge under such circumstances are less than those from running away, or from stopping and giving battle in unfavorable terrain following the enemy's attack.

CHAPTER XIV
TRAINING

THE SCOPE OF TRAINING

Training is not limited to the military arts; we must also pay attention to political training, to the literacy movement, to training in hygiene, etc. Consequently, when a guerrilla unit is engaged in drill, literacy training should represent an appropriate part of the whole, and can be given in all places and at all times.

For the purpose of achieving a full and satisfactory result from all the kinds of training carried out in a guerrilla unit, we must increase the will to study on their own initiative among the officers and soldiers. Apart from the political aspect, and in addition to increasing political consciousness, we must also promote amusements for the army, mitigate a painful and tedious existence, assist the people in their own self-defense, and cause the armed force of the popular masses to unite closely with us.

TRAINING IN ALL SUBJECTS

The consequence of training in all subjects, though it is difficult to reduce it to uniformity, is, as regards methods in general, to proceed from the superficial to the profound, first the broad and then the rigorous, from the simple and easy to the complex and difficult, first the partial and then the universal. In all fields, one must demonstrate one's theories by concrete experience, so as to strengthen the students' confidence.

CULTIVATING THE PEOPLE'S CAPACITY FOR SELF-DEFENSE

The most pressing and most important task of a guerrilla unit is to carry out guerrilla attacks without ceasing in the places occupied by the enemy, to seize and kill all traitors and reactionaries, and to protect the popular masses. At the same time, a guerrilla unit must investigate the concrete offenses of the enemy and use every possible method to discover and smash his tricks and plots. Therefore:

1. It is advantageous to make known our good government, to make great efforts to unite with the popular masses, and to support the forces of the popular masses. Such actions can also be carried out on the territory of the enemy. We should also use every possible method and devote all our strength to encourage the people to imitate our own actions, stimulate them to fight the enemy actively, and guide their combat.

2. Our action in supporting the people's capacity for self-defense should be of long duration, and not ephemeral. We must do the best we can to let people know that, at all times, a guerrilla unit struggles and sacrifices itself for the popular masses and, even in the case of the most dangerous crisis, will absolutely not harm the popular masses. If the local population meets with a defeat in its first military action, after we have drawn it into the war, its spirit of struggle will necessarily be dissipated to some extent. When the masses falter in this way, we must devise a way to rouse their enthusiasm and to bring their spirit of struggle to a high level once more.

3. A guerrilla unit constitutes the most conscious and advanced segment of the people. Hence, they should first unite those among the popular masses who are dissatisfied with the enemy and who accept the leadership of those we send among them.

We must also aid the people to establish plans, to get arms, and to establish liaison and mutual assistance with mass organizations in neighboring villages and even in other cities that are victims of the enemy's oppression. But, in carrying out all such work, we must maintain the strictest secrecy.

TRAINING IN HYGIENE

1. In order to strengthen its own fighting capacity, every mess unit should designate one or two soldiers as nurses, to treat the ailments of the officers and soldiers when they arise and, also to explain the rudiments of hygiene, as well as to assist, direct, supervise, and encourage all matters of hygiene in the unit.

2. Replenishing stocks of medicines is an extremely difficult matter in a guerrilla unit. Hence we should, in accordance with the seasons etc., prepare certain medicines especially for emergency care, and other normally indispensable medicines. As regards wounded and seriously ill members of the unit, when there is no alternative, they are entrusted to fellow soldiers with some slight medical knowledge or to local inhabitants sympathetic to us.

MILITARY TRAINING

Military training all relates to the enemy army. Its purpose is to create greater skill than that of the enemy in each specialized art.

1. Subjects. The items requiring particular attention are dispersing, assembling, marksmanship, maneuvering an army, mountain climbing, construction of military works, night fighting, mountain fighting, fighting on narrow roads, espionage and security measures, searches, liaison, and other such actions.

2. Methods. In carrying out military instruction, particular attention should be paid to all methods of teaching and explanation, which should be more or less as described below:

    a. For theoretical instruction one can employ the method of giving suggestions and the method of questions and answers. All methods of teaching that adopt the style of speechmaking and injecting [ideas into the students' heads] should be eliminated in so far as possible.

    b. When explaining actions, we should pay attention to linking our talks with the living reality, so that it will be easy for the soldiers to understand us.

    c. We should devote more time to concrete demonstrations of actions and less time to talking about empty theories. Consequently, the greatest effort should be made to diminish the duration and number of classroom sessions and the numbers of practical exercises should be increased.

    d. All explanations in the classroom should in so far as possible correspond to the exercises outside.

    e. All demonstrations of actions should be carefully prepared in advance before they are executed. All negligent and perfunctory behavior—doing things any old way—must absolutely be eliminated.

    f. With respect to all activities, we should devise a way to incite the officers and soldiers to carry out a competition, in order to increase the spirit of initiative and the positive attitude they manifest in their work, and to speed up the work.

    g. Increase applied training, diminish training according to a fixed pattern, and correct the erroneous idea that training according to a fixed pattern is useful in maintaining military discipline.

    h. The plan of training should be suited to the circumstances, time, and place in which it is to be carried out. The training plan must absolutely not be rigid; we must seize every occasion and strive to give training adapted to the circumstances. This is done more or less as indicated below:

i. We utilize the time when the army is on the march to carry on direction finding, recognizing differences in terrain, estimating distances, reconnaissance action, and designating objectives and the utilization of terrain.

j. When we are in camp, we utilize preparations for security measures in order to carry out exercises in all kinds of observation and precautions, beginning with the role of advanced sentries. We also provide training in construction of military works.

k. We utilize the opportunity provided by a battle, and before setting out or before the fighting begins, we explain, on the basis of the tasks we have been ordered to perform, such forms of action as ambushes, surprise attacks, main attacks, and supporting attacks, etc.

l. We utilize the opportunity, when we are waiting the moment for action, to explain in practical terms how we resist the charges of the enemy, as well as shooting and other such military actions.

m. We utilize post-battle exposition and criticism (such exposition and criticism should be based on a minute investigation of the facts, carried out beforehand) to point out the strength and weaknesses in our actions during the battle and what was appropriate and inappropriate in the individual commands, thus giving a concrete lesson to all of officers and men.

n. We utilize the time offered by morning and evening roll calls to give various kinds of talks.

o. We utilize the occasion offered by the recreation period to put on games, dances, and modern-style plays, having military significance, thus imperceptibly increasing the officers' and soldiers' desire to correct themselves, and increasing their willingness to follow good examples.

p. We utilize each occasion of reward and punishment to carry out thorough propaganda among the officers and soldiers, in order to increase the soldiers' sense of achievement and their shame in doing evil, and thus, little by little, fostering a good military discipline.

POLITICAL TRAINING

In order to assure that all the independent actions of a guerrilla unit attain complete victory, apart from reinforcing military training, the most important thing is that we must make certain that the officers and soldiers have a high level of "political consciousness" and of "devotion" to their own cause. Political training is the only method by which this objective can be attained. Its content is described in detail later on.

THE LITERACY MOVEMENT

In order to increase the cultural level of the officers and soldiers, so that they may more easily absorb all kinds of training, each mess unit must carry out literacy training. The methods are as follows:

1. The "A" class includes all those who know about fifty characters.

2. The "B" class includes those who know above twenty characters.

3. The "C" class includes those who know no characters at all.

4. The teachers of the various classes consist of those in the unit with a relatively high cultural level.

5. When we halt, there should be an hour each day devoted to the study of characters. When we are on the march, we can carry out instruction either while moving or during rest periods. In such training, the important thing is regularity rather than speed. In general, if the soldiers learn two words a day, it is excellent.

CHAPTER XV
POLITICAL WORK

THE AIM OF THE POLITICAL WORK OF A GUERRILLA UNIT

This aim lies in strengthening and raising to a higher level the fighting capacity of each member of the unit. The fighting capacity of a guerrilla unit is not determined exclusively by military arts, but depends above all on political consciousness, political influence, setting in motion the broad popular masses, disintegrating the enemy army, and inducing the broad popular masses to accept our leadership. All the plans of a guerrilla unit, whether they be political. military, or of any other nature, are all directed toward this single end.

THE MAIN CONTENT OF POLITICAL WORK

We must carry out political instruction directed toward the resurrection of our people (stimulate the soldiers' national consciousness, their patriotism, and their love for the people and for the masses) and see to it that every officer and soldier in a guerrilla unit understands not only the national tasks for which he is responsible but also the necessity of fighting in defense of our state.

We must also pay attention to supporting the leaders, to maintaining the solidarity of the unit with real sincerity, to carrying out to the end the orders of one's superiors, and to maintaining an iron military discipline. We must see to it that the multitude of the soldiers are of a single mind and endowed with the resolve and the will to save our country together.

Apart from strengthening its own fighting capacity, a guerrilla unit must also carry out propaganda among the masses regarding the plots of the invaders and of the enemy.

DISCUSSIONS IN SMALL GROUPS

These are excellent activities to unite our walls, to strengthen confidence, and to proclaim our doctrine.

1. We collect the view of all the comrades, in order to avoid feelings of alienation and to achieve the effect of gathering together ideas and obtaining greater advantage.

2. By the cadres, we increase their capacity for work and give them more practice in techniques for holding meetings and in methods of speaking. We will also be able to solve problems more quickly, investigate the past, and transform the future.

3. We can thus verify the fellowship existing among the members of the unit, and draw new comrades into the party.

4. This method is convenient for training, and makes it possible to understand completely each comrade's circumstances, capacity, and knowledge.

5. According to their character, these activities can be divided into discussion meetings, review meetings, and criticism meetings.

METHODS

Before the meeting we must prepare for it. These preparations consist in informing the members of the group, establishing the essential subject matter of the discussion, and, at the same time, reporting to the next higher echelon.

1. As regards the number of participants, from three to five represents the optimum.

2. One should not be bound by any rigid pattern. Discussion meetings can be held at all times and in all places.

3. As for the time limit, it is not desirable that the meetings should last too long. One hour is the maximum permissible.

4. It is appropriate to hold one meeting a week. The order of procedure consists in a report by the chairman, discussion of the report by the participants, and a conclusion entrusted to the leader of the group. The record of the meeting should indicate in detail the name of the chairman, the subjects of discussion, the number of those present and absent, and the place where the meeting was held.

5. Not more than two problems at most should be discussed. The discussion should have as its starting point the individual problems of the participants.

6. As for the manner of speaking, it is appropriate that the remarks of the participants should deal with essentials and be simple and clear. They should be systematic and not repetitive. They should be persuasive in content and presented in a friendly and agreeable manner. In answering questions, one should avoid any hint of mockery and pay attention to what the others say. At the same time, one should arrive at a decision concerning the topic discussed.

7. As regards the leader of the group, his report should be simple. He should not give a long and repetitive presentation but seize the occasion to induce the participants to speak.

Mao Zedong

8. The conclusion should follow the inductive method. It should include a criticism of the whole of the discussions. If there are dissident conclusions, they may also be expressed

CARRYING OUT POLITICAL WORK

One should not merely rely on a few political workers. The best thing is to be able to attract and train conscious elements, or interested officers and soldiers, to participate in the work and to train the whole personnel of the unit so that they can all carry on effective political work.

TYPES OF POLITICAL WORK

In broad terms, political work can be divided into three categories according to whether it is carried out in ordinary times, during battle, or after a battle. As for propaganda destined to encourage the troops, the various aspects are as indicated below:

1. Political work in ordinary times. We intensify political training in order to raise the level of political consciousness, create unity in thought, word, and deed, maintain an iron military discipline, and unite closely with the popular masses. The methods are roughly as follows:

   a. We must really put into practice the principles of not disturbing or harming the people (such as "Pay fairly for what you buy," "Speak politely," "Return everything you borrow", and "Pay for anything you damage").
   b. At all times and in all places, aid the popular masses and help them to solve their difficulties (for example, help the popular masses to gather the harvest or to cultivate their land and send our army doctors to prevent epidemics or treat the people's ailments, or to

enquire after people who have suffered difficulties and devise methods to aid them), maintain the unity of the army and the people, and encourage the spirit of sharing both good fortune and adversity together.

c. Chat frequently with the popular masses and let them know about our military discipline and our affection for them, and also learn in detail about the hunger and suffering among the people.

d. Frequently hold joint entertainment sessions for the soldiers and the people, so as to smooth over any feelings of alienation between the army and the people and increase the affection of the army and the people for one another.

2. Resolving any feelings of alienation between the lower and higher ranks of officers and soldiers. The methods employed are roughly as follows:

a. Persons engaged in political training, apart from sharing the good fortune and adversity of the soldiers, should also frequently chat with the soldiers, carefully investigate all their deep grieves and report their problems at all times to their superior officers, and devise methods for improving the situation.

b. As regards all the opinions of higher and lower ranks, we should take our stand on a position of pure rational knowledge, convince them by an attitude of sincere entreaty, and explain things to them. We must make absolutely certain that higher and lower ranks unite solidly as one man, and we must strengthen their capacity to unite.

c. With respect to soldiers who violate discipline, we should use educational methods to persuade them. All corporal punishment and insults must absolutely be reduced.

d. We should frequently hold meetings at which officers and soldiers can enjoy themselves together, in order to heighten the affection between officers and soldiers.

3. Augmenting the officers' and soldiers' hatred of the enemy, and increasing their resolve to fight to the death to kill the enemy. Increasing the common hatred of the enemy is an important factor in strengthening the soldiers' morale. Consequently, a guerrilla unit should pay particular attention to all the atrocities of the enemy, and to all the instances in which he massacres our army or our people, and carry out propaganda generally among the army regarding these atrocities, so as to heighten the courage of the officers and soldiers to fight to the death and harden their resolve to fight the enemy to the death, since either we or they must perish.

4. Strengthening confidence in the inevitable victory of our war against the enemy. The methods are more or less as follows:

a. We must frequently avail ourselves of the tales of the glorious feats of arms in our past, in order to carry out propaganda among our officers and soldiers and inspire them.

b. We put forward examples of the enemy's defects (such as difficulties, collapses, and other problems that he has recently encountered), in order to demonstrate that in the end the enemy must be defeated.

c. We must put forward examples of our own strong points (such as the support of the popular masses, transmission of information, familiarity with the terrain) and the present victorious circumstances, in order to demonstrate that we must ultimately triumph.

d. By exposing the clever tricks habitually used by the enemy, we make known the points to which our army should pay particular attention, in order to prevent the emergence of a mentality of fearing or underestimating the enemy.

After we have suffered an attack, we sink for a time into a situation characterized by difficulties and painful effort, and as a consequence we underestimate ourselves, exaggerate the enemy's strength, and lose our confidence in victory.

POLITICAL WORK IN TIME OF BATTLE

Political work before we set out is carried on as described below.

1. The commander in chief of the unit first calls a meeting of the cadres. He explains in what respects the existing political situation is favorable to us, as well as the conditions of victory and the significance of the battle. He also explains the methods and points for attention in attaining our goal, but without infringing military secrecy.

2. On the basis of the meeting of the cadres, the political training section immediately calls meetings of political workers at all levels, at which the essential points and the methods of propaganda are explained and concrete tasks are assigned.

3. The various groups immediately call meetings of all the officers and soldiers, at which, in addition to reporting on the current political situation and the guarantees of our victory, conditions for competition are also put forward. ("He who is lightly wounded should not leave the firing line, he who is seriously wounded should not cry out in pain"; "Let us see who can hand in the most weapons"; or "Let us see who can take the most prisoners,") At the same time, tasks are distributed to all political workers and activists (supervision, leadership, or propaganda).

4. Political workers should be sent to the local population to gather them together, call meetings, and give talks, inspiring them to participate in the battle or to join the ranks of the porters or the transport units. As regards the organizations of the popular masses, we should guide them in methods of calling meetings, of fighting, and of preparing mobilization.

5. After the battle has begun, the most important political training workers should be sent to inspire the units responsible for the main attack or for particularly important actions. The less important political training workers should be sent to inspire the less important fighting units.

6. Propaganda units and groups of singers and dancers (all composed of lively and lovable boys in uniform and attractive clothing) should be sent in advance to positions along the side of the roads where the army will advance, to give short talks, sing, dance, or shout slogans, so as to inspire the maximum of courage in the officers and soldiers.

POLITICAL WORK AFTER THE BATTLE HAS BEGUN

1. After the battle has begun, we should pay attention to calling out slogans to the soldiers of the other side, so as to dissipate their morale. This is one of the forms taken by our work of sabotage.

2. When the situation on the battlefield enters the stage of an encounter at close range or from positions arrayed opposite one another, we devise a method for holding a joint meeting with the soldiers of the opposite side and take advantage of this opportunity to give them food, in order to gladden their hearts. After this, we carry on more propaganda work, which must be prepared in advance.

3. After the battle has begun, we must assuredly carry out propaganda directed toward those outside our army. It is even more important to inspire those within our army. The methods for this work are diverse and are determined primarily by what is adapted to the circumstances. For example:

A. On the attack:

   i.   When we suffer a surprise attack by the enemy while advancing to attack, we should give an explanation such as the following "Comrades! Airplanes cannot decide a battle. We must seize this opportunity, advance rapidly, and quickly come to grips with the enemy on the ground. Charge the enemy with your bayonets!"

   ii.   When firing begins, we should encourage the soldiers in the following terms: "Comrades! Don't shoot at random, shoot only when you have taken careful aim. We must try to kill an enemy with every bullet."

   iii. When we are near the enemy and are about to charge, the method for inspiring the soldiers is as follows: "Comrades! The time to dispose of the enemy has come. We shall pay no attention to sacrifice, we shall summon up our courage, defeat the enemy and annihilate him. Let our victory inspire the whole army! Forward quickly! Charge!"

   iv. When the first charge is repelled and we charge a second time, we should encourage the soldiers as follows: "Comrades! We are an invincible iron army, we are a mighty unit victorious in every battle, we are absolutely resolved to destroy this enemy and preserve our glorious reputation."

   v.   When officers are wounded or killed in battle, we should exhort the troops as follows: "Comrades! Our officers (So-and-so) and (So-and-so) have already sacrificed themselves gloriously. Let us tread in their bloody footsteps, complete their task, and annihilate the enemy before us. Let us go and avenge them!"

vi. If the enemy shows signs of wavering, we should exhort the soldiers as follows: "Comrades! The enemy is wavering. Charge quickly and capture his commander in chief alive!"

vii. When we pursue the enemy, we should exhort the soldiers as follows: "Comrades! The enemy has retreated. Pursue him quickly! Charge and smash the enemy's holding units, finish off his main force, annihilate his whole force. Let us see who can hand in the most arms, and who can take the most prisoners. To win a battle and not to pursue the enemy is a great pity."

B. On the defense:

i. When the order has been received, we should carry out propaganda as follows: "Comrades! The enemy has arrived. This is the best opportunity to annihilate the enemy. Make skillful use of natural obstacles, and shoot with *sang-froid*. The more of the enemy we kill and wound, the easier it will be for our main attack to progress and obtain results."

ii. When the enemy charges, we should exhort the troops as follows: "Comrades! The enemy is about to charge. Fix your bayonets, and prepare your hand grenades. Let us summon up our awe-inspiring reputation, preserve the glory we have already won, and annihilate the enemy in front of our position."

iii. When we are surrounded by the enemy, we should exhort the soldiers as follows: "Comrades! We are an ever-victorious unit. We are a courageous and invincible iron army. We will wage a bloody battle to the end for our people and our country, shed our last drop of blood, hold onto our rifles to the death, and die rather than surrender. To hand over one's rifle is suicide, to surrender is the supreme shame. Let us smash their lines at one point and break through."

iv.   At the time of the counterattack or when the order to go over to the offensive is received: "Comrades! We are counterattacking. Let us take away the enemy's rifles, let us capture the enemy officers, let us see who is most courageous!"

v.   Propaganda when we retreat: "Comrades! Let us keep our movements secret and baffle the enemy in his calculations. Let us open wide our arms and lure the enemy to penetrate deep. Do not break ranks, do not fall behind, do not waver, do not succumb to panic, do not fear sacrifice, execute resolutely to the end the orders of your superiors. Final victory will be ours!"

vi.   When we cover the withdrawal of our forces, the methods for exhorting them are similar to those indicated above.

POLITICAL WORK FOLLOWING A BATTLE

After the battle has been concluded, political work continues.

1. In order to avoid the appearance of attitudes of slighting the enemy or fearing the enemy, we should pay attention to the following points:

a.   We should correctly point out the causes of victory and defeat. We must not become puffed up because of a small victory; still less can we lose our confidence in victory because of a small setback.

    b. We must establish the attitude that should be adopted henceforth, or the points requiring attention.

2. We should collect materials and anecdotes concerning our victory, as well as the names of units, individual officers, and soldiers who have fought courageously. We should then use these materials to compose propaganda outlines, songs, dances, old- and new-style plays, etc.

3. We should print large numbers of victory announcements and slogans and stick them up everywhere. At the same time, we should organize a roving propaganda unit, which spreads out toward areas established in advance, to carry out propaganda and to call the popular masses together and hold meetings to celebrate the victory.

4. When meetings are held to celebrate the victory, one should pay attention to the following points:

    a. Report on the significance of the victory, and the tasks now before us, as well as the concrete methods to be employed to carry out these tasks.
    b. Report on units that have fought courageously, as well as individual officers and soldiers. As for officers and soldiers wounded or killed, one can select the most valuable among them and report about them.
    c. Put on new versions of classic plays, as well as songs and dances.

While the reports indicated under "a" and "b" above are being delivered, or the play is being put on, the units participating in such a meeting should shout out slogans in accompaniment.

We should also bring up the methods for providing pensions to the members of the families of the soldiers killed in battle.

Moreover, we should bring together the prisoners and booty in the sight of the masses, thus further increasing the courage and the spirit of struggle of our soldiers and of the people.

5. At meetings to celebrate the victory, all organizations should also launch a consolation movement. The main points for attention in this respect are:

     a. As regards material consolation, the important thing is not the quantity, but the significance; it is not the elegance and refinement of the items given, but their utility. Such things as straw sandals, face towels, pigs, sheep, chickens, and ducks are all suitable for this purpose.

     b. In case there is a lack of goods for material consolation, consolation in the form of honors should be used. For example, one can make flags for presentation, or compose songs in memory of the fallen, or issue an order of the day in their praise.

     c. Following a small victory, there should be no large-scale consolation. Consolation should be carried out only if we can devise means for doing it in a place near the battlefield.

6. We should praise examples of combined operations, autonomous actions, and the resolute application of orders. Thus:

     a. When there are those who, in the course of a fierce battle, have achieved victory by combined operations, autonomous action, and the resolute execution of orders, the maximum effort should be made to publicize the fact and to praise them. Those who have the misfortune to be defeated in similar circumstances should also be praised.

b. When there is punishment for those who, in order to preserve their own forces, fail to advance, or fail to carry out their tasks energetically, thus bringing about the defeat of another unit of our army, the case should also be the object of large-scale propaganda within the unit. In this way we give a lesson to the officers and soldiers of the whole unit, or of other units, and make them afraid to commit similar offenses.

WORK PERTAINING TO CLUBS AND AMUSEMENT ROOMS

By virtue of the fact that it compensates for a painful and tedious existence in the army, this is also a way of preventing desertion. The essentials regarding the organization and work of clubs are dealt with below.

1. Rules regarding organization.

a. In order to promote entertainment in the army, compensate for a tedious existence, increase interest in our work, and inspire a taste for study, each mess unit within a guerrilla unit should organize an amusement room, This should be divided into a military section, a guerrilla section, and a physical culture section. Each officer and soldier in the mess unit should choose one of these sections, in accordance with his own nature; he can, if he wishes, participate in two or three of the sections.

b. One person from among the company commanders or the particularly energetic and capable platoon commanders should be chosen to be responsible for the amusement room. Each of the three sections should have a section head, chosen at a meeting of the members of the section, for a period of six months with the possibility of being chosen to succeed himself.

c. Each week there should be one meeting of the section heads and one meeting of the members of each section. A meeting of the leaders should be held once a month. It is called separately by the chairman of the section heads.

d. In its work, the amusement room should follow the guidance of the club of the next higher echelon. It is also subject to the supervision and guidance of the commanding officer of the unit. In military affairs, it is absolutely subordinate to the commanding officer of the unit.

e. In order to guide and unify the work of the various amusement rooms, a guerrilla battalion should establish a club. This club should have a chairman and a secretary who are responsible for all its activities.

f. The club should be attached to the political training section, because the work of the amusement rooms constitutes a kind of political training. If there is no political training section, the club is directly subordinated to the commanding of officer.

g. The work of the club consists in guiding and promoting the work of the various amusement rooms. Consequently, each week there should be a meeting of the responsible heads of the various amusement rooms, and each month we should call a meeting of all the officers and soldiers or a meeting of the army and the people together.

All the work of both the clubs and amusement rooms should have as its principle not to interfere with military administration, military training, or military action.

2. The essentials of the work of clubs and amusement rooms.

a. The work of the military section consists in furthering a spirit of independent study among the officers and soldiers, in discussion of military questions, or in the mutual rectification of the actions of the members in order to remedy the lacks and insufficiencies of military training. Its content is as indicated below.

i. Bayonet section (practice, taking a hypothetical enemy dummy as the object).

ii. Grenade section (throwing a wooden hand grenade at a target).

b. Guerrilla section.

i. Taking aim from a fixed support.

ii. Checking one's aim.

iii. Carriage while shooting.

iv. Investigations when setting out.

v. Utilization of obstacles.

vi. Shooting at various types of objectives in the field.

3. Physical culture section. The work of this section lies in strengthening the bodies of the officers and soldiers. It can also remedy insufficiencies in military training. Its contents are as follows:

    a. Ball playing (basketball, football, volley ball, tennis, baseball, etc.).
    b. Track and field sports (high jump, broad jump, races, obstacle course).
    c. Boxing and swordplay.

4. Entertainment section. The work of this section consists in providing amusement for the members of the army, in compensating for a tedious existence, and in increasing the soldiers' interest in their work and their taste for study.

a. Joke section. This section can carry on its activities at any time at all, but attention should be paid to the following points:

i. When jokes are told, we must make them easy to understand. We can take materials from joke books and such, but they should not be too obscene.

ii. When telling stories, we should devote much time to stories about the abundant exploits and great enterprises of the ancients, and to their excellent words and admirable conduct, in order to achieve an inspirational effect.

iii. When reporting on the news, we should devote attention to our own victories and to the atrocities of the enemy.

b. Theatrical section. This section utilizes rest periods, both in the evenings and during the day, to put on all sorts of new-style plays, traditional operas, comedy teams, storytellers with drums, etc.—performances that have political content and are at the same time amusing, in order to improve morale.

c. Song and dance section. In accordance with the circumstances in which the unit finds itself and the nature of its tasks, this section composes all sorts of songs in order to stimulate the interest of the officers and soldiers in singing songs, or it puts on dances in costume, assuming various comical attitudes, in order to make the onlookers laugh until they hold their sides.

d. Music section. This is divided into violin, harmonica, guitar and other groups, which can accompany the plays and dances.

e. The methods of work of all sections should be adapted to the time and circumstances. They should be employed in a lively manner, and on no account in a wooden fashion.

f. The work of all sections should be subject to strict control and supervision. We should also use methods of competition to induce all the officers and soldiers to make spontaneous efforts.

g. All kinds of songs and old and new plays, etc.

h. For the benefit of the work, all groups and sections should have specialized talents.

i. The officers and soldiers who participate in these performances should be excused from their other duties.

F

COLLECTED WRITINGS
OF
CHAIRMAN MAO

POLITICS AND TACTICS

PART 2

ON CORRECTING
MISTAKEN IDEAS
IN THE PARTY

Mao Zedong

Preface

December, 1929

This article was a resolution drawn up by Comrade Mao Zedong for the Ninth Party Congress of the Fourth Army of the Red Army. The building of the Chinese people's armed forces was a difficult process.

The Chinese Red Army (which became the Eighth Route and New Fourth Armies during the War of Resistance against Japan and is now the People's Liberation Army) was created on August 1, 1927, during the Nanchang Uprising, and by December 1929 had been in existence for over two years. During this period the Communist Party organization in the Red army learned a great deal and gained quite a rich store of experience in the course of combating various mistaken ideas.

ON CORRECTING MISTAKEN IDEAS IN THE PARTY

There are various non-proletarian ideas in the Communist Party organization in the Fourth Red Army which greatly hinder the application of the Party's correct line. Unless these ideas are thoroughly corrected, the Fourth Army cannot possibly shoulder the tasks assigned to it in China's great revolutionary struggle. The source of such incorrect ideas in this Party organization lies, of course, in the fact that its basic units are composed largely of peasants and other elements of petty-bourgeois origin; yet the failure of the Party's leading bodies to wage a concerted and determined struggle against these incorrect ideas and to educate the members in the Party's correct line is also an important cause of their existence and growth. In accordance with the spirit of the September letter of the Central Committee, this congress hereby points out the manifestations of various non-proletarian ideas in the Party organization in the Fourth Army, their sources, and the methods of correcting them, and calls upon all comrades to eliminate them thoroughly.

ON THE PURELY MILITARY VIEWPOINT

The purely military viewpoint is very highly developed among a number of comrades in the Red Army. It manifests itself as follows:

1. These comrades regard military affairs and politics as opposed to each other and refuse to recognize that military affairs are only one means of accomplishing political tasks. Some even say, "If you are good militarily, naturally you are good politically; if you are not good militarily, you cannot be any good politically"--this is to go a step further and give military affairs a leading position over politics.

2. They think that the task of the Red Army like that of the White Army, is merely to fight. They do not understand that the Chinese Red Army is an armed body for carrying out the political tasks of the revolution. Especially at present, the Red Army should certainly not confine itself to fighting; besides fighting to destroy the enemy's military strength, it should shoulder such important tasks as doing propaganda among the masses, organizing the masses, arming them, helping them to establish revolutionary political power and setting up Party organizations. The Red Army fights not merely for the sake of fighting but in order to conduct propaganda among the masses, organize them, arm them, and help them to establish revolutionary political power. Without these objectives, fighting loses its meaning and the Red Army loses the reason for its existence.

3. Hence, organizationally, these comrades subordinate the departments of the Red Army doing political work to those doing military work, and put forward the slogan, "Let Army Headquarters handle outside matters." If allowed to develop, this idea would involve the danger of estrangement from the masses, control of the government by the army and departure from proletarian leadership-- it would be to take the path of warlordism like the Kuomintang army.

4. At the same time, in propaganda work they overlook the importance of propaganda teams. On the question of mass organization, they neglect the organizing of soldiers' committees in the army and the organizing of the local workers and peasants. As a result, both propaganda and organizational work are abandoned.

5. They become conceited when a battle is won and dispirited when a battle is lost.

6. Selfish departmentalism--they think only of the Fourth Army and do not realize that it is an important task of the Red Army to arm the local masses.

7. Unable to see beyond their limited environment in the Fourth Army, a few comrades believe that no other revolutionary forces exist. Hence their extreme addiction to the idea of conserving strength and avoiding action. This is a remnant of opportunism.

8. Some comrades, disregarding the subjective and objective conditions, suffer from the malady of revolutionary impetuosity; they will not take pains to do minute and detailed work among the masses, but, riddled with illusions, want only to do big things. This is a remnant of putschism.[1]

The sources of the purely military viewpoint are:

1. A low political level. From this flows the failure to recognize the role of political leadership in the army and to recognize that the Red Army and the White army are fundamentally different.

2. The mentality of mercenaries. Many prisoners captured in past battles have joined the Red Army, and such elements bring with them a markedly mercenary outlook, thereby providing a basis in the lower ranks for the purely military viewpoint.

3. From the two preceding causes there arises a third, overconfidence in military strength and absence of confidence in the strength of the masses of the people.

4 The Party's failure actively to attend to and discuss military work is also a reason for the emergence of the purely military viewpoint among a number of comrades.

The methods of correction are as follows:

1. Raise the political level in the Party by means of education, destroy the theoretical roots of the purely military viewpoint, and be dear on the fundamental difference between the Red Army and the White army. At the same time, eliminate the remnants of opportunism and putschism and break down the selfish departmentalism of the Fourth Army.

2. Intensify the political training of officers and men and especially the education of ex-prisoners. At the same time, as far as possible let the local governments select workers and peasants experienced in struggle to join the Red Army, thus organizationally weakening or even eradicating the purely military viewpoint.

3. Arouse the local Party organizations to criticize the Party organizations in the Red Army and the organs of mass political power to criticize the Red Army itself, in order to influence the Party organizations and the officers and men of the Red Army.

4. The Party must actively attend to and discuss military work. All the work must be discussed and decided upon by the Party before being carried out by the rank and file.

5. Draw up Red Army rules and regulations which dearly define its tasks, the relationship between its military and its political apparatus, the relationship between the Red Army and the masses of the people, and the powers and functions of the soldiers' committees and their relationship with the military and political organizations.

ON ULTRA-DEMOCRACY

Since the Fourth Army of the Red Army accepted the directives of the Central Committee, there has been a great decrease in the manifestations of ultra-democracy. For example, Party decisions are now carried out fairly well; and no longer does anyone bring up such erroneous demands as that the Red Army should apply "democratic centralism from the bottom to the top" or should "let the lower levels discuss all problems first, and then let the higher levels decide". Actually, however, this decrease is only temporary and superficial and does not mean that ultra-democratic ideas have already been eliminated. In other words, ultra-democracy is still deep-rooted in the minds of many comrades. Witness the various expressions of reluctance to carry out Party decisions.

The methods of correction are as follows:

1. In the sphere of theory, destroy the roots of ultra-democracy. First, it should be pointed out that the danger of ultra-democracy lies in the fact that it damages or even completely wrecks the Party organization and weakens or even completely undermines the Party's fighting capacity, rendering the Party incapable of fulfilling its fighting tasks and thereby causing the defeat of the revolution. Next, it should be pointed out that the source of ultra-democracy consists in the petty bourgeoisie's individualistic aversion to discipline. When this characteristic is brought into the Party, it develops into ultra-democratic ideas politically and organizationally. These ideas are utterly incompatible with the fighting tasks of the proletariat.

2. In the sphere of organization, ensure democracy under centralized guidance. It should be done on the following lines:

a. The leading bodies of the Party must give a correct line of guidance and kind solutions when problems arise, in order to establish themselves as centers of leadership.
b. The higher bodies must be familiar with the life of the masses and with the situation in the lower bodies so as to have an objective basis for correct guidance.
c. No Party organization at any level should make casual decisions in solving problems. Once a decision is reached, it must be firmly carried out.
d. All decisions of any importance made by the Party's higher bodies must be promptly transmitted to the lower bodies and the Party rank and file. The method is to call meetings of activists or general membership meetings of the Party branches or even of the columns[2], and to assign people to make reports at such meetings.
e. The lower bodies of the Party and the Party rank and file must discuss the higher bodies' directives in detail in order to understand their meaning thoroughly and decide on the methods of carrying them out.

ON THE DISREGARD OF ORGANIZATIONAL DISCIPLINE

Disregard of organizational discipline in the Party organization in the Fourth Army manifests itself as follows:

A. Failure of the minority to submit to the majority. For example, when a minority finds its motion voted down, it does not sincerely carry out the Party decisions.

The methods of correction are as follows:

1. At meetings, all participants should be encouraged to voice their opinions as fully as possible. The rights and wrongs in any controversy should be clarified without

compromise or glossing over. In order to reach a clear-cut conclusion, what cannot be settled at one meeting should be discussed at another, provided there is no interference with the work.

2. One requirement of Party discipline is that the minority should submit to the majority. If the view of the minority has been rejected, it must support the decision passed by the majority. If necessary, it can bring up the maker for reconsideration at the next meeting, but apart from that it must not act against the decision in any way.

B. Criticism made without regard to organizational discipline:

1. Inner-Party criticism is a weapon for strengthening the Party organization and increasing its fighting capacity. In the Party organization of the Red Army, however, criticism is not always of this character, and sometimes turns into personal attack. As a result, it damages the Party organization as well as individuals. This is a manifestation of petty-bourgeois individualism. The method of correction is to help Party members understand that the purpose of criticism is to increase the Party's fighting capacity in order to achieve victory in the class struggle and that it should not be used as a means of personal attack.

2. Many Party members make their criticisms not inside, but outside, the Party. The reason is that the general membership has not yet grasped the importance of the Party organization (its meetings and so forth), and sees no difference between criticism inside and outside the organization. The method of correction is to educate Party members so that they understand the importance of Party organization and make their criticisms of Party committees or comrades at Party meetings.

ON ABSOLUTE EQUALITARIANISM

Absolute equalitarianism became quite serious in the Red Army at one time. Here are some examples. On the matter of allowances to wounded soldiers, there were objections to differentiating between light and serious cases, and the demand was raised for equal allowances for all. When officers rode on horseback, it was regarded not as something necessary for performing their duties but as a sign of inequality. Absolutely equal distribution of supplies was demanded, and there was objection to somewhat larger allotments in special cases. In the hauling of rice, the demand was made that all should carry the same load on their backs, irrespective of age or physical condition. Equality was demanded in the allotment of billets, and the Headquarters would be abused for occupying larger rooms. Equality was demanded in the assignment of fatigue duties, and there was unwillingness to do a little more than the next man. It even went so far that when there were two wounded men but only one stretcher, neither could be carried away because each refused to yield priority to the other. Absolute equalitarianism, as shown in these examples, is still very serious among officers and soldiers of the Red Army.

Absolute equalitarianism, like ultra-democracy in political matters, is the product of a handicraft and small peasant economy--the only difference being that the one manifests itself in material affairs, while the other manifests itself in political affairs.

The method of correction: We should point out that, before the abolition of capitalism, absolute equalitarianism is a mere illusion of peasants and small proprietors, and that even under socialism there can be no absolute equality, for material things will then be distributed on the principle of "from each according to his ability, to each according to his work" as well as on that of meeting the needs of the work. The distribution of material things in the Red Army must be more or less equal, as in the case of equal pay for officers and men, because this is required by the present circumstances of the struggle. But absolute equalitarianism beyond reason must be opposed because it is not required by the struggle; on the contrary, it hinders the struggle.

ON SUBJECTIVISM

Subjectivism exists to a serious degree among some Party members, causing great harm to the analysis of the political situation and the guidance of the work. The reason is that subjective analysis of a political situation and subjective guidance of work inevitably result either in opportunism or in putschism. As for subjective criticism, loose and groundless talk or suspiciousness, such practices inside the Party often breed unprincipled disputes and undermine the Party organization.

Another point that should be mentioned in connection with inner-Party criticism is that some comrades ignore the major issues and confine their attention to minor points when they make their criticism. They do not understand that the main task of criticism is to point out political and organizational mistakes. As to personal shortcomings, unless they are related to political and organizational mistakes, there is no need to be overcritical and to embarrass the comrades concerned. Moreover, once such criticism develops, there is the great danger that the Party members will concentrate entirely on minor faults, and everyone will become timid and overcautious and forget the Party's political tasks.

The main method of correction is to educate Party members so that a political and scientific spirit pervades their thinking and their Party life. To this end we must: (1) teach Party members to apply the Marxist-Leninist method in analyzing a political situation and appraising the class forces, instead of making a subjective analysis and appraisal; (2) direct the attention of Party members to social and economic investigation and study, so as to determine the tactics of struggle and methods of work, and help comrades to understand that without investigation of actual conditions they will fall into the pit of fantasy and putschism; and (3) in inner-Party criticism, guard against subjectivism, arbitrariness and the vulgarization of criticism; statements should be based on facts and criticism should centre on politics.

ON INDIVIDUALISM

The tendency towards individualism in the Red Army Party organization manifests itself as follows:

1. Retaliation. Some comrades, after being criticized inside the Party by a soldier comrade, look for opportunities to retaliate outside the Party, and one way is to beat or abuse the comrade in question. They also seek to retaliate within the Party. "You have criticized me at this meeting, so I'll find some way to pay you back at the next." Such retaliation arises from purely personal considerations, to the neglect of the interests of the class and of the Party as a whole. Its target is not the enemy class, but individuals in our own ranks. It is a corrosive which weakens the organization and its fighting capacity.
2. "Small group" mentality. Some comrades consider only the interests of their own small group and ignore the general interest. Although on the surface this does not seem to be the pursuit of personal interests, in reality it exemplifies the narrowest individualism and has a

strong corrosive and centrifugal effect. "Small group" mentality used to be rife in the Red Army, and although there has been some improvement as a result of criticism, there are still survivals and further effort is needed to overcome it.

3. The "employee" mentality. Some comrades do not understand that the Party and the Red Army, of which they are members, are both instruments for carrying out the tasks of the revolution. They do not realize that they themselves are makers of the revolution, but think that their responsibility is merely to their individual superiors and not to the revolution. This passive mentality of an "employee" of the revolution is also a manifestation of individualism. It explains why there are not very many activists who work unconditionally for the revolution. Unless it is eliminated, the number of activists will not grow and the heavy burden of the revolution will remain on the shoulders of a small number of people, much to the detriment of the struggle.

4. Pleasure-seeking. In the Red Army there are also quite a few people whose individualism finds expression in pleasure-seeking. They always hope that their unit will march into big cities. They want to go there not to work but to enjoy themselves. The last thing they want is to work in the Red areas where life is hard.

5. Passivity. Some comrades become passive and stop working whenever anything goes against their wishes. This is mainly due to lack of education, though sometimes it is also due to the leadership's improper conduct of affairs, assignment of work or enforcement of discipline.

6. The desire to leave the army. The number of people who ask for transfers from the Red Army to local work is on the increase The reason for this does not lie

entirely with the individuals but also with: (1) the material hardships of life in the Red Army, (2) exhaustion after long struggle, and (3) the leadership's improper conduct of affairs, assignment of work or enforcement of discipline.

The method of correction is primarily to strengthen education so as to rectify individualism ideologically. Next, it is to conduct affairs, make assignments and enforce discipline in a proper way. In addition, ways must be found to improve the material life of the Red Army, and every available opportunity must be utilized for rest and rehabilitation in order to improve material conditions. In our educational work we must explain that in its social origin individualism is a reflection within the Party of petty-bourgeois and bourgeois ideas.

ON THE IDEOLOGY OF ROVING REBEL BANDS

The political ideology of roving rebel bands has emerged in the Red Army because the proportion of vagabond elements is large and because there are great masses of vagabonds in China, especially in the southern provinces. This ideology manifests itself as follows: (1) Some people want to increase our political influence only by means of roving guerrilla actions, but are unwilling to increase it by undertaking the arduous task of building up base areas and establishing the people's political power. (2) In expanding the Red Army, some people follow the line of "hiring men and buying horses" and "recruiting deserters and accepting mutineers", [3] rather than the line of expanding the local Red Guards and the local troops and thus developing the main forces of the Red Army. (3) Some people lack the patience to carry on arduous struggles together with the masses, and only want to go to the big cities to eat and drink to their hearts' content. All these manifestations of the ideology of roving rebels seriously hamper the Red Army in performing its proper tasks; consequently its eradication is an important objective in the ideological struggle within the Red Army Party organization. It must be understood that the ways of roving rebels of the Huang Chao [4] or Li Chuang [5] type are not permissible under present-day conditions.

The methods of correction are as follows:

1. Intensify education, criticize incorrect ideas, and eradicate the ideology of roving rebel bands.

2. Intensify education among the basic sections of the Red Army and among recently recruited captives to counter the vagabond outlook.

3. Draw active workers and peasants experienced in struggle into the ranks of the Red Army so as to change its composition.

4. Create new units of the Red Army from among the masses of militant workers and peasants.

ON THE REMNANTS OF PUTSCHISM

The Party organization in the Red Army has already waged struggles against putschism, but not yet to a sufficient extent. Therefore, remnants of this ideology still exist in the Red Army. Their manifestations are: (1) blind action regardless of subjective and objective conditions; (2) inadequate and irresolute application of the Party's policies for the cities; (3) slack military discipline, especially in moments of defeat; (4) acts of house-burning by some units; and (5) the practices of shooting deserters and of inflicting corporal punishment, both of which smack of putschism. In its social origins, putschism is a combination of *lumpen*-proletarian and petty- bourgeois ideology.

The methods of correction are as follows:

1. Eradicate putschism ideologically.

2. Correct putschist behavior through rules, regulations and policies.

NOTES

1. For a brief period after the defeat of the revolution in 1927, a "Left" putschist tendency arose in the Communist Party. Regarding the Chinese revolution as a "permanent revolution" and the revolutionary situation in China as a "permanent upsurge", the putschist comrades refused to organize an orderly retreat and, adopting the methods of commandism and relying only on a small number of Party members and a small section of the masses, erroneously attempted to stage a series of local uprisings throughout the country, which had no prospect of success. Such putschist activities were widespread at the end of 1927 but gradually subsided in the beginning of 1928, though sentiments in favor of putschism still survived among some comrades.

2 In the guerrilla system of organization a column corresponded to a division in the regular army, with a complement much more flexible and usually much smaller than that of a regular division.

3 These two Chinese idioms refer to the methods which some rebels in Chinese history adopted to expand their forces. In the application of these methods, attention was paid to numbers rather than to quality, and people of all sorts were indiscriminately recruited to swell the ranks.

4 Huang Chao was the leader of the peasant revolts towards the end of the Tang Dynasty. In A.D. 875, starting from his home district Tsaochow (now Hotse County in Shantung), Huang led armed peasants in victorious battles against the imperial forces and styled himself the "Heaven-Storming General". In the course of a decade he swept over most of the provinces in the Yellow, Yangtse, Huai and Pearl river valleys, reaching as far as Kwangsi. He finally broke through the Tungkuan pass,

Mao Zedong

captured the imperial capital of Changan (now Sian in Shensi), and was crowned Emperor of Chi. Internal dissensions and attacks by the non-Han tribal allies of the Tang forces compelled Huang to abandon Changan and retreat to his native district, where he committed suicide. The ten years' war fought by him is one of the most famous peasant wars in Chinese history. Dynastic historians record that "all people suffering from heavy taxes and levies rallied to him". But as he merely carried on roving warfare without ever establishing relatively consolidated base areas, his forces were called "roving rebel bands".

5 Li Chuang, short for Li Tzu-cheng the King Chuang (the Dare-All King), native of Michih, northern Shensi, was the leader of a peasant revolt which led to the overthrow of the Ming Dynasty. The revolt first started in northern Shensi in 1628. Li joined the forces led by Kao Ying-hsiang and campaigned through Honan and Anhwei and back to Shensi. After Kao's death in 1636, Li succeeded him, becoming King Chuang, and campaigned in and out of the provinces of Shensi, Szechuan, Honan and Hupeh Finally he captured the imperial capital of Peking in 1644, whereupon the last Ming emperor committed suicide. The chief slogan he spread among the masses was "Support King Chuang, and pay no grain taxes". Another slogan of his to enforce discipline among his men ran: "Any murder means the killing of my father, any rape means the violation of my mother." Thus he won the support of the masses and his movement became the main current of the peasant revolts raging all over the country. As he, too, roamed about without ever establishing relatively consolidated base areas, he was eventually defeated by Wu San-kuei, a Ming general who colluded with the Ching troops in a joint attack on Li.

Mao Zedong

COLLECTED WRITINGS
OF
CHAIRMAN MAO

POLITICS AND TACTICS

PART 3

THE CHINESE
REVOLUTION
AND
THE CHINESE
COMMUNIST PARTY

Preface

December 1939

The Chinese Revolution and the Chinese Communist Party is a textbook which was written jointly by Comrade Mao Zedong and several other comrades in Yenan to the winter of 1939.

The first chapter, "Chinese Society", was drafted by other comrades and revised by Comrade Mao Zedong. The second chapter, "The Chinese Revolution", was written by Comrade Mao Zedong himself. Another chapter, scheduled to deal with "Party Building", was left unfinished by the comrades working on it. The two published chapters, and especially Chapter II, have played a great educational role in the Chinese Communist Party and among the Chinese people. The views on New Democracy set out by Comrade Mao Zedong in Chapter II were considerably developed in his "On New Democracy", written in January 1940.

*The current population of China in 2009 is estimated to be 1.4 billion, as opposed to the 1939 figure of 450 million referenced in this essay.

CHAPTER I
CHINESE SOCIETY

THE CHINESE NATION

China is one of the largest countries in the world, her territory being about the size of the whole of Europe. In this vast country of ours there are large areas of fertile land which provide us with food and clothing; mountain ranges across its length and breadth with extensive forests and rich mineral deposits; many rivers and lakes which provide us with water transport and irrigation; and a long coastline which facilitates communication with nations beyond the seas. From ancient times our forefathers have labored, lived and multiplied on this vast territory.

China borders on the Union of Soviet Socialist Republics in the northeast, the northwest and part of the west; the Mongolian People's Republic in the north; Afghanistan, India, Bhutan and Nepal in the southwest and part of the west; Burma and Indo-China in the south; and Korea in the east, where she is also a close neighbor of Japan and the Philippines. China's geographical setting has its advantages and disadvantages for the Chinese people's revolution. It is an advantage to be adjacent to the Soviet Union and fairly distant from the major imperialist countries in Europe and America, and to have many colonial or semi-colonial countries around us. It is a disadvantage that Japanese imperialism, making use of its geographical proximity, is constantly threatening the very existence of all China's nationalities and the Chinese people's revolution.

China has a population of 450 million, or almost a quarter of the world total. Over nine-tenths of her inhabitants belong to the Han nationality. There are also scores of minority nationalities, including the Mongol, Hui, Tibetan, Uighur, Miao, Yi, Chuang, Chungchia and Korean nationalities, all with long histories though at different levels of cultural development. Thus China is a country with a very large population composed of many nationalities.

Developing along the same lines as many other nations of the world, the Chinese people (here we refer mainly to the Hans) went through many thousands of years of life in classless primitive communes. Some 4,000 years have gone by since the collapse of these primitive communes and the transition to class society, which took the form first of slave and then of feudal society. Throughout the history of Chinese civilization its agriculture and handicrafts have been renowned for their high level of development; there have been many great thinkers, scientists, inventors, statesmen, soldiers, men of letters and artists, and we have a rich store of classical works. The compass was invented in China very long ago. [1] The art of paper-making was discovered as early as 1,800 years ago. [2] Block-printing was invented 1,300 years ago, [3] and movable type 800 years ago. [4] The use of gunpowder was known to the Chinese before the Europeans. [5] Thus China has one of the oldest civilizations in the world; she has a recorded history of nearly 4,000 years.

The Chinese nation is known throughout the world not only for its industriousness and stamina, but also for its ardent love of freedom and its rich revolutionary traditions. The history of the Han people, for instance, demonstrates that the Chinese never submit to tyrannical rule but invariably use revolutionary means to overthrow or change it. In the thousands of years of Han history, there have been hundreds of peasant uprisings, great and small, against the dark rule of the landlords and the nobility. And most dynastic changes came about as a result of such peasant uprisings. All the nationalities of China have resisted foreign oppression and have invariably resorted to rebellion to shake it off. They favor a union on the basis of equality but are against the oppression of one nationality by another. During the thousands of years of recorded history, the Chinese nation has given birth to many national heroes and revolutionary leaders. Thus the Chinese nation has a glorious revolutionary tradition and a splendid historical heritage.

THE OLD FEUDAL SOCIETY

Although China is a great nation and although she is a vast country with an immense population, a long history, a rich revolutionary tradition and a splendid historical heritage, her economic, political and cultural development was sluggish for a long time after the transition from slave to feudal society. This feudal society, beginning with the Chou and Chin Dynasties, lasted about 3,000 years.

The main features of the economic and political system of China's feudal era were as follows:

1. A self-sufficient natural economy predominated. The peasants produced for themselves not only agricultural products but most of the handicraft articles they needed. What the landlords and the nobility exacted from them in the form of land rent was also chiefly for private enjoyment and not for exchange. Although exchange developed as time went on, it did not play a decisive role in the economy as a whole.

2. The feudal ruling class composed of landlords, the nobility and the emperor owned most of the land, while the peasants had very little or none at all. The peasants tilled the land of the landlords, the nobility and the royal family with their own farm implements and had to turn over to them for their private enjoyment 40, 50, 60,

Collected Writings of Chairman Mao: Politics and Tactics

70, or even 80 per cent or more of the crop. In effect the peasants were still serfs.

3. Not only did the landlords, the nobility and the royal family live on rent extorted from the peasants, but the landlord state also exacted tribute, taxes and *corvee* services from them to support a horde of government officials and an army which was used mainly for their repression.

4. The feudal landlord state was the organ of power protecting this system of feudal exploitation. While the feudal state was torn apart into rival principalities in the period before the Chin Dynasty, it became autocratic and centralized after the first Chin emperor unified China, though some feudal separatism remained. The emperor reigned supreme in the feudal state, appointing officials in charge of the armed forces, the law courts, the treasury and state granaries in all parts of the county and relying on the landed gentry as the mainstay of the entire system of feudal rule.

It was under such feudal economic exploitation and political oppression that the Chinese peasants lived like slaves, in poverty and suffering, through the ages. Under the bondage of feudalism they had no freedom of person. The landlord had the right to beat, abuse or even kill them at will, and they had no political rights whatsoever. The extreme poverty and backwardness of the peasants resulting from ruthless landlord exploitation and oppression is the basic reason why Chinese society remained at the same stage of socio-economic development for several thousand years.

The principal contradiction in feudal society was between the peasantry and the landlord class.

The peasants and the handicraft workers were the basic classes which created the wealth and culture of this society.

The ruthless economic exploitation and political oppression of the Chinese peasants forced them into numerous uprisings against landlord rule. There were hundreds of uprisings, great and small, all of them peasant revolts or peasant revolutionary wars--from the uprisings of Chen Sheng, Wu Kuang, Hsiang Yu and Liu Pang [6] in the Chin Dynasty, those of Hsinshih, Pinglin, the Red Eyebrows, the Bronze Horses [7] and the Yellow Turbans [8] in the Han Dynasty, those of Li Mi and Tou Chien-the [9] in the Sui Dynasty, those of Wang Hsienchih and Huang Chao [10] in the Tang Dynasty, those of Sung Chiang and Fang La [11] in the Sung Dynasty, that of Chu Yuan-chang [12] the Yuan Dynasty, and that of Li Tzu-cheng [13] in the Ming Dynasty, down to the uprising known as the War of the Taiping Heavenly Kingdom in the Ching Dynasty. The scale of peasant uprisings and peasant wars in Chinese history has no parallel anywhere else. The class struggles of the peasants, the peasant uprisings and peasant wars constituted the real motive force of historical development in Chinese feudal society. For each of the major peasant uprisings and wars dealt a blow to the feudal regime of the time, and hence more or less furthered the growth of the social productive forces. However, since neither new productive forces, nor new relations of production, nor new class forces, nor any advanced political party existed in those days, the peasant uprisings and wars did not have correct leadership such as the proletariat and the Communist Party provide today; every peasant revolution failed, and the peasantry was invariably used by the landlords and the nobility, either during or after the revolution, as a lever for bringing about dynastic change. Therefore' although some social progress was made after each great peasant revolutionary struggle, the feudal economic relations and political system remained basically unchanged.

It is only in the last hundred years that a change of a different order has taken place.

PRESENT-DAY COLONIAL, SEMI-COLONIAL AND SEMI-FEUDAL SOCIETY

As explained above, Chinese society remained feudal for 3,000 years. But is it still completely feudal today? No, China has changed. After the Opium War of 1840 China gradually changed into a semi-colonial and semi-feudal society. Since the Incident of September 18 1931, when the Japanese imperialists started their armed aggression, China has changed further into a colonial, semi-colonial and semi-feudal society. We shall now describe the course of this change.

As discussed in Section 2, Chinese feudal society lasted for about 3,000 years. It was not until the middle of the 19th century, with the penetration of foreign capitalism, that great changes took place in Chinese society.

As China's feudal society had developed a commodity economy, and so carried within itself the seeds of capitalism, China would of herself have developed slowly into a capitalist society even without the impact of foreign capitalism. Penetration by foreign capitalism accelerated this process. Foreign capitalism played an important part in the disintegration of China's social economy, on the one hand it undermined the foundations of her self-sufficient natural economy and wrecked the handicraft industries both in the cities and in the peasants' homes, and on the other, it hastened the growth of a commodity economy in town and country.

Apart from its disintegrating effects on the foundations of China's feudal economy, this state of affairs gave rise to certain objective conditions and possibilities for the development of capitalist production in China. For the destruction of the natural economy created a commodity market for capitalism, while the bankruptcy of large numbers of peasants and handicraftsmen provided it with a labor market

In fact, some merchants, landlords and bureaucrats began investing in modern industry as far back as sixty years ago, in the latter part of the 19th century, under the stimulus of foreign capitalism and because of certain cracks in the feudal economic structure. About forty years ago, at the turn of the century, China's national capitalism took its first steps forward. Then about twenty years ago, during the first imperialist world war, China's national industry expanded, chiefly in textiles and flour milling, because the imperialist countries in Europe and America were preoccupied with the war and temporarily relaxed their oppression of China.

The history of the emergence and development of national capitalism is at the same time the history of the emergence and development of the Chinese bourgeoisie and proletariat. Just as a section of the merchants, landlords and bureaucrats were precursors of the Chinese bourgeoisie, so a section of the peasants and handicraft workers were the precursors of the Chinese proletariat. As distinct social classes, the Chinese bourgeoisie and proletariat are new-born and never existed before in Chinese history. They have evolved into new social classes from the womb of feudal society. They are twins born of China's old (feudal) society, at once linked to each other and antagonistic to each other. However, the Chinese proletariat emerged and grew simultaneously not only with the Chinese national bourgeoisie but also with the enterprises directly operated by the imperialists in China. Hence, a very large section of the Chinese proletariat is older and more experienced than the Chinese bourgeoisie, and is therefore a greater and more broadly based social force.

However, the emergence and development of capitalism is only one aspect of the change that has taken place since the imperialist penetration of China. There is another concomitant and obstructive aspect, namely, the collusion of imperialism with the Chinese feudal forces to arrest the development of Chinese capitalism.

It is certainly not the purpose of the imperialist powers invading China to transform feudal China into capitalist China. On the contrary, their purpose is to transform China into their own semi-colony or colony.

To this end the imperialist powers have used and continue to use military, political, economic and cultural means of oppression, so that China has gradually become a semi-colony and colony. They are as follows:

1. The imperialist powers have waged many wars of aggression against China, for instance, the Opium War launched by Britain in 1840, the war launched by the Anglo-French allied forces in 1857, [14] the Sino-French War of 1884, [15] the Sino-Japanese War of 1894, and the war launched by the allied forces of the eight powers in 1900. [16] After defeating China in war, they not only occupied many neighboring countries formerly under her protection, but seized or "leased" parts of her territory. For instance, Japan occupied Taiwan and the Penghu Islands and "leased" the port of Lushun, Britain seized Hong Kong and France "leased" Kwangchowwan. In addition to

annexing territory, they exacted huge indemnities. Thus heavy blows were struck at China's huge feudal empire.

2. The imperialist powers have forced China to sign numerous unequal treaties by which they have acquired the right to station land and sea forces and exercise consular jurisdiction in China, [17] and they have carved up the whole country into imperialist spheres of influence. [18]

3. The imperialist powers have gained control of all the important trading ports in China by these unequal treaties and have marked off areas in many of these ports as concessions under their direct administration. [19] They have also gained control of China's customs, foreign trade and communications (sea, land, inland water and air). Thus they have been able to dump their goods in China, turn her into a market for their industrial products, and at the same time subordinate her agriculture to their imperialist needs.

4. The imperialist powers operate many enterprises in both light and heavy industry in China in order to utilize her raw materials and cheap labor on the spot, and they thereby directly exert economic pressure on China's national industry and obstruct the development of her productive forces.

5. The imperialist powers monopolize China's banking and finance by extending loans to the Chinese government and establishing banks in China. Thus they have not only overwhelmed China's national capitalism in commodity competition, they have also secured a stranglehold on her banking and finance.

6. The imperialist powers have established a network of comprador and merchant-usurer exploitation right across China, from the trading ports to the remote hinterland, and have created a comprador and merchant-usurer class in their service, so as to facilitate

their exploitation of the masses of the Chinese peasantry and other sections of the people.

7. The imperialist powers have made the feudal landlord class as well as the comprador class the main props of their rule in China. Imperialism "first allies itself with the ruling strata of the previous social structure, with the feudal lords and the trading and money-lending bourgeoisie, against the majority of the people. Everywhere imperialism attempts to preserve and to perpetuate all those pre-capitalist forms of exploitation (especially in the villages) which serve as the basis for the existence of its reactionary allies". [20] "Imperialism, with all its financial and military might, is the force in China that supports, inspires, fosters and preserves the feudal survivals, together with their entire bureaucratic-militarist superstructure." [21]

8. The imperialist powers supply the reactionary government with large quantities of munitions and a host of military advisers, in order to keep the warlords fighting among themselves and to suppress the Chinese people.

9. Furthermore, the imperialist powers have never slackened their efforts to poison the minds of the Chinese people. This is their policy of cultural aggression. And it is carried out through missionary work, through establishing hospitals and schools, publishing newspapers and inducing Chinese students to study abroad. Their aim is to train intellectuals who will serve their interests and to dupe the people.

10. Since September 18, 1931, the large-scale invasion of Japanese imperialism has turned a big chunk of semi-colonial China into a Japanese colony.

These facts represent the other aspect of the change that has taken place since the imperialist penetration of China--the blood-stained picture of feudal China being reduced to semi-feudal, semi-colonial and colonial China.

It is thus clear that in their aggression against China the imperialist powers have on the one hand hastened the disintegration of feudal society and the growth of elements of capitalism, thereby transforming a feudal into a semi-feudal society, and on the other imposed their ruthless rule on China, reducing an independent country to a semi-colonial and colonial country.

Taking both these aspects together, we can see that China's colonial, semi-colonial and semi-feudal society possesses the following characteristics:

1. The foundations of the self-sufficient natural economy of feudal times have been destroyed, but the exploitation of the peasantry by the landlord class, which is the basis of the system of feudal exploitation, not only remains intact but, linked as it is with exploitation by comprador and usurer capital, clearly dominates China's social and economic life.
2. National capitalism has developed to a certain extent and has played a considerable part in China's political and cultural life but it has not become the principal pattern in China's social economy, it is flabby and is mostly associated with foreign imperialism and domestic feudalism in varying degrees.
3. The autocratic rule of the emperors and nobility has been overthrown, and in its place there have arisen first the warlord-bureaucrat rule of the landlord class and then the joint dictatorship of the landlord class and the big bourgeoisie. In the occupied areas there is the rule of Japanese imperialism and its puppets.

4. Imperialism controls not only China's vital financial and economic arteries but also her political and military power. In the occupied areas everything is in the hands of Japanese imperialism.

5. China's economic, political and cultural development is very uneven, because she has been under the complete or partial domination of many imperialist powers, because she has actually been in a state of disunity for a long time, and because her territory is immense.

6. Under the twofold oppression of imperialism and feudalism and especially as a result of the large-scale invasion of Japanese imperialism, the Chinese people, and particularly the peasants, have become more and more impoverished and have even been pauperized in large numbers, living in hunger and cold and without any political rights. The poverty and lack of freedom among the Chinese people are on a scale seldom found elsewhere.

Such are the characteristics of China's colonial, semi-colonial and semi-feudal society.

This situation has in the main been determined by the Japanese and other imperialist forces; it is the result of the collusion of foreign imperialism and domestic feudalism.

The contradiction between imperialism and the Chinese nation and the contradiction between feudalism and the great masses of the people are the basic contradictions in modern Chinese society. Of course, there are others, such as the contradiction between the bourgeoisie and the proletariat and the contradictions within the reactionary ruling classes themselves. But the contradiction between imperialism and the Chinese nation is the principal one.

These contradictions and their intensification must inevitably result in the incessant growth of revolutionary movements. The great revolutions in modern and contemporary China have emerged and grown on the basis of these basic contradictions.

CHAPTER II
THE CHINESE REVOLUTION

THE REVOLUTIONARY MOVEMENTS IN THE LAST HUNDRED YEARS

The history of China's transformation into a semi-colony and colony by imperialism in collusion with Chinese feudalism is at the same time a history of struggle by the Chinese people against imperialism and its lackeys. The Opium War, the Movement of the Taiping Heavenly Kingdom, the Sino-French War, the Sino-Japanese War, the Reform Movement of 1898, the Yi Ho Tuan Movement, the Revolution of 1911, the May 4th Movement, the May 30th Movement, the Northern Expedition, the Agrarian Revolutionary War and the present War of Resistance Against Japan--all testify to the Chinese people's indomitable spirit in fighting imperialism and its lackeys.

Thanks to the Chinese people's unrelenting and heroic struggle during the last hundred years, imperialism has not been able to subjugate China, nor will it ever be able to do so.

The valiant Chinese people will certainly fight on, even though Japanese imperialism is now exerting its full strength in an all-out offensive and many landlord and big bourgeois elements, such as the overt and covert Wang Ching-weis, have already capitulated to the enemy or are preparing to do so. This heroic struggle will not cease until the Chinese people have driven Japanese imperialism out of China and achieved the complete liberation of the country.

The national revolutionary struggle of the Chinese people has a history of fully one hundred years counting from the Opium War of 1840, or of thirty years counting from the Revolution of

1911. It has not yet run its full course, nor has it yet performed its tasks with any signal success; therefore the Chinese people, and above all the Communist Party, must shoulder the responsibility of resolutely fighting on

What are the targets of the revolution? What are its tasks? What are its motive forces? What is its character? And what are its perspectives? These are the questions we shall now deal with.

THE TARGETS OF THE CHINESE REVOLUTON

From our analysis in the third section of Chapter I, we know that present-day Chinese society is a colonial, semi-colonial and semi-feudal society. Only when we grasp the nature of Chinese society will we be able clearly to understand the targets, tasks, motive forces and character of the Chinese revolution and its perspectives and future transition. A clear understanding of the nature of Chinese society, that is, of Chinese conditions, is therefore the key to a clear understanding of all the problems of the revolution.

Since the nature of present-day Chinese society is colonial, semi-colonial and semi-feudal, what are the chief targets or enemies at this stage of the Chinese revolution?

They are imperialism and feudalism, the bourgeoisie of the imperialist countries and the landlord class of our country. For it is these two that are the chief oppressors, the chief obstacles to the progress of Chinese society at the present stage. The two collude with each other in oppressing the Chinese people, and imperialism is the foremost and most ferocious enemy of the Chinese people, because national oppression by imperialism is the more onerous.

Since Japan's armed invasion of China, the principal enemy of the revolution has been Japanese imperialism together with all the Chinese traitors and reactionaries in league with it, whether they have capitulated openly or are preparing to do so.

The Chinese bourgeoisie, which is also a victim of imperialist oppression, once led or played a principal role in revolutionary struggles such as the Revolution of 1911, and has participated in revolutionary struggles such as the Northern Expedition and the present War of Resistance Against Japan. In the long period from 1927 to 1937, however, its upper stratum, namely, the section represented by the reactionary clique within the Kuomintang, collaborated with imperialism, formed a reactionary alliance with the landlord class, betrayed the friends who had helped it--the Communist Party, the proletariat, the peasantry and other sections of the petty bourgeoisie--betrayed the Chinese revolution and brought about its defeat. At that time therefore, the revolutionary people and the revolutionary political party (the Communist Party) could not but regard these bourgeois elements as one of the targets of the revolution. In the War of Resistance a section of the big landlord class and big bourgeoisie, represented by Wang Ching-wei, has turned traitor and deserted to the enemy. Consequently, the anti-Japanese people cannot but regard these big bourgeois elements who have betrayed our national interests as one of the targets of the revolution.

It is evident, then, that the enemies of the Chinese revolution are very powerful. They include not only powerful imperialists and powerful feudal forces, but also, at times, the bourgeois reactionaries who collaborate with the imperialist and feudal forces to oppose the people. Therefore, it is wrong to underestimate the strength of the enemies of the revolutionary Chinese people.

In the face of such enemies, the Chinese revolution cannot be other than protracted and ruthless. With such powerful enemies, the revolutionary forces cannot be built up and tempered into a power capable of crushing them except over a long period of time. With enemies who so ruthlessly suppress the Chinese revolution, the revolutionary forces cannot hold their own positions, let alone capture those of the enemy, unless they steel themselves and display their tenacity to the full. It is therefore wrong to think that the forces of the Chinese revolution can be built up in the twinkling of an eye, or that China's revolutionary struggle can triumph overnight.

In the face of such enemies, the principal means or form of the Chinese revolution must be armed struggle, not peaceful struggle. For our enemies have made peaceful activity impossible for the Chinese people and have deprived them of all political freedom and democratic rights. Stalin says, "In China the armed revolution is fighting the armed counter-revolutionary. That is one of the specific features and one of the advantages of the Chinese revolution."[22] This formulation is perfectly correct. Therefore, it is wrong to belittle armed struggle, revolutionary war, guerrilla war and army work.

In the face of such enemies, there arises the question of revolutionary base areas. Since China's key cities have long been occupied by the powerful imperialists and their reactionary Chinese allies, it is imperative for the revolutionary ranks to turn the backward villages into advanced, consolidated base areas, into great military, political, economic and cultural bastions of the revolution from which to fight their vicious enemies who are using the cities for attacks on the rural districts, and in this way gradually to achieve the complete victory of the revolution through protracted fighting; it is imperative for them to do so if they do not wish to compromise with imperialism and its lackeys but are determined to fight on, and if they intend to build up and temper their forces, and avoid decisive battles with a powerful enemy while their own strength is inadequate. Such being the case, victory in the Chinese revolution can be won first in the rural areas and this is possible because China's economic development is uneven (her economy not being a unified capitalist economy), because her territory is extensive (which gives the revolutionary forces room to maneuver), because the counter-revolutionary camp is disunited and full of contradictions, and because the struggle of the peasants who are the main force in the revolution is led by the Communist Party, the party of the proletariat; but on the other hand, these very circumstances make the revolution uneven and render the task of winning complete victory protracted and arduous. Clearly then the protracted revolutionary struggle in the revolutionary base areas consists mainly in peasant guerrilla warfare led by the Chinese Communist Party. Therefore, it is wrong to ignore the necessity of using rural districts as revolutionary base areas, to neglect painstaking work among the peasants, and to neglect guerrilla warfare.

However, stressing armed struggle does not mean abandoning other forms of struggle; on the contrary, armed struggle cannot succeed unless co-ordinated with other forms of struggle. And stressing the work in the rural base areas does not mean abandoning our work in the cities and in the other vast rural areas which are still under the enemy's rule; on the contrary, without the work in the cities and in these other rural areas, our own rural base areas would be isolated and the revolution would suffer defeat. Moreover, the final objective of the revolution is the capture of the cities, the enemy's main bases, and this objective cannot be achieved without adequate work in the cities.

It is thus clear that the revolution cannot triumph either in the rural areas or in the cities without the destruction of the enemy's army, its chief weapon against the people. Therefore, besides annihilating the enemy's troops in battle, there is the important task of disintegrating them.

It is also clear that the Communist Party must not be impetuous and adventurist in its propaganda and organizational work in the urban and rural areas which have been occupied by the enemy and dominated by the forces of reaction and darkness for a long time but that it must have well-selected cadres working underground, must accumulate strength and bide its time there. In leading the people in struggle against the enemy, the Party must adopt the tactics of advancing step by step slowly and surely, keeping to the principle of waging struggles on just grounds, to our advantage, and with restraint, and making use of such open forms of activity as are permitted by law, decree and social custom; empty clamor and reckless action can never lead to success.

THE TASKS OF THE CHINESE REVOLUTION

Imperialism and the feudal landlord class being the chief enemies of the Chinese revolution at this stage, what are the present tasks of the revolution?

Unquestionably, the main tasks are to strike at these two enemies, to carry out a national revolution to overthrow foreign imperialist oppression and a democratic revolution to overthrow feudal landlord oppression, the primary and foremost task being the national revolution to overthrow imperialism.

These two great tasks are interrelated. Unless imperialist rule is overthrown, the rule of the feudal landlord class cannot be terminated, because imperialism is its main support. Conversely, unless help is given to the peasants in their struggle to overthrow the feudal landlord class, it will be impossible to build powerful revolutionary contingents to overthrow imperialist rule, because the feudal landlord class is the main social base of imperialist rule in China and the peasantry is the main force in the Chinese revolution. Therefore the two fundamental tasks, the national revolution and the democratic revolution, are at once distinct and united.

In fact, the two revolutionary tasks are already linked, since the main immediate task of the national revolution is to resist the Japanese imperialist invaders and since the democratic revolution must be accomplished in order to win the war. It is wrong to regard the national revolution and the democratic revolution as two entirely different stages of the revolution.

THE MOTIVE FORCES OF THE CHINESE REVOLUTION

Given the nature of Chinese society and the present targets and tasks of the Chinese revolution as analyzed and defined above, what are the motive forces of the Chinese revolution?

Since Chinese society is colonial, semi-colonial and semi-feudal, since the targets of the revolution are mainly foreign imperialist rule and domestic feudalism, and since its tasks are to overthrow these two oppressors, which of the various classes and strata in Chinese society constitute the forces capable of fighting them? This is the question of the motive forces of the Chinese revolution at the present stage. A clear understanding of this question is indispensable to a correct solution of the problem of the basic tactics of the Chinese revolution.

What classes are there in present-day Chinese society? There are the landlord class and the bourgeoisie, the landlord class and the upper stratum of the bourgeoisie constituting the ruling classes in Chinese society. And there are the proletariat, the peasantry, and the different sections of the petty bourgeoisie other than the peasantry, all of which are still the subject classes in vast areas of China.

The attitude and the stand of these classes towards the Chinese revolution are entirely determined by their economic status in society. Thus the motive forces as well as the targets and tasks of the revolution are determined by the nature of China's socio-economic system.

Let us now analyze the different classes in Chinese society.

1. The Landlord Class

The landlord class forms the main social base for imperialist rule in China; it is a class which uses the feudal system to exploit and oppress the peasants, obstructs China's political, economic and cultural development and plays no progressive role whatsoever.

Therefore, the landlords, as a class, are a target and not a motive force of the revolution.

In the present War of Resistance a section of the big landlords, along with one section of the big bourgeoisie (the capitulationists), has surrendered to the Japanese aggressors and turned traitor, while another section of the big landlords, along with another section of the big bourgeoisie (the die-hards), is increasingly wavering even though it is still in the anti-Japanese camp. But a good many of the enlightened gentry who are middle and small landlords and who have some capitalist coloration display some enthusiasm for the war, and we should unite with them in the common fight against Japan,

2. The Bourgeoisie

There is a distinction between the comprador big bourgeoisie and the national bourgeoisie.

The comprador big bourgeoisie is a class which directly serves the capitalists of the imperialist countries and is nurtured by them; countless ties link it closely with the feudal forces in the countryside. Therefore, it is a target of the Chinese revolution and never in the history of the revolution has it been a motive force.

However, different sections of the comprador big bourgeoisie owe allegiance to different imperialist powers, so that when the contradictions among the latter become very acute and the revolution is directed mainly against one particular imperialist power, it becomes possible for the sections of the comprador class which serve other imperialist groupings to join the current anti-imperialist front to a certain extent and for a certain period. But they will turn against the Chinese revolution the moment their masters do.

In the present war the pro-Japanese big bourgeoisie (the capitulationists) have either surrendered or are preparing to surrender. The pro-European and pro-American big bourgeoisie (the die-hards) are wavering more and more, even though they are still in the anti-Japanese camp, and they are playing the double game of simultaneously resisting Japan and opposing the Communist Party. Our policy towards the big bourgeois capitulationists is to treat them as enemies and resolutely strike them down. Towards the big bourgeois die-hards, we employ a revolutionary dual policy; on the one hand, we unite with them because they are still anti-Japanese and we should make use of their contradictions with Japanese imperialism, but on the other hand, we firmly struggle against them because they pursue a high-handed anti-Communist, reactionary policy detrimental to resistance and unity, both of which would be jeopardized without such a struggle.

The national bourgeoisie is a class with a dual character.

On the one hand, it is oppressed by imperialism and fettered by feudalism and consequently is in contradiction with both of them. In this respect it constitutes one of the revolutionary forces. In the course of the Chinese revolution it has displayed a certain enthusiasm for fighting imperialism and the governments of bureaucrats and warlords.

But on the other hand, it lacks the courage to oppose imperialism and feudalism thoroughly because it is economically and politically flabby and still has economic ties with imperialism and feudalism. This emerges very clearly when the people's revolutionary forces grow powerful.

It follows from the dual character of the national bourgeoisie that, at certain times and to a certain extent, it can take part in the revolution against imperialism and the governments of bureaucrats and warlords and can become a revolutionary force, but that at other times there is the danger of its following the comprador big bourgeoisie and acting as its accomplice in counter-revolution.

The national bourgeoisie in China, which is mainly the middle bourgeoisie, has never really held political power but has been restricted by the reactionary policies of the big landlord class and big bourgeoisie which are in power, although it followed them in opposing the revolution in the period from 1927 to 1931 (before the September 18th Incident). In the present war, it differs not only from the capitulationists of the big landlord class and big bourgeoisie but also from the big bourgeois die-hards, and so far has been a fairly good any of ours. Therefore, it is absolutely necessary to have a prudent policy towards the national bourgeoisie.

3. The Different Sections of the Petty Bourgeoisie Other than the Peasantry

The petty bourgeoisie, other than the peasantry, consists of the vast numbers of intellectuals, small tradesmen, handicraftsmen and professional people.

Their status somewhat resembles that of the middle peasants, they all suffer under the oppression of imperialism, feudalism and the big bourgeoisie, and they are being driven ever nearer to bankruptcy or destitution.

Hence these sections of the petty bourgeoisie constitute one of the motive forces of the revolution and are a reliable ally of the proletariat. Only under the leadership of the proletariat can they achieve their liberation.

Let us now analyze the different sections of the petty bourgeoisie other than the peasantry.

First, are the intellectuals and student youth. They do not constitute a separate class or stratum. In present-day China most of them may be placed in the petty-bourgeois category, judging by their family origin, their living conditions and their political outlook. Their numbers have grown considerably during the past few decades. Apart from that section of the intellectuals which has associated itself with the imperialists and the big bourgeoisie and works for them against the people, most intellectuals and students are oppressed by imperialism, feudalism and the big bourgeoisie, and live in fear of unemployment or of having to discontinue their studies.

Therefore, they tend to be quite revolutionary. They are more or less equipped with bourgeois scientific knowledge, have a keen political sense and often play a vanguard role or serve as a link with the masses in the present stage of the revolution. The movement of the Chinese students abroad before the Revolution of 1911, the May 4th Movement of 1919, the May 30th Movement of 1925 and the December 9th Movement of 1935 are striking proofs of this. In particular, the large numbers of more or less impoverished intellectuals can join hands with the workers and peasants in supporting or participating in the revolution. In China, it was among the intellectuals and young students that Marxist-Leninist ideology was first widely disseminated and accepted. The revolutionary forces cannot be successfully organized and revolutionary work cannot be successfully conducted without the participation of revolutionary intellectuals. But the intellectuals often tend to be subjective and individualistic, impractical in their thinking and irresolute in action until they have thrown themselves heart and soul into mass revolutionary struggles, or made up their minds to serve the interests of the masses and become one with them. Hence although the mass of revolutionary intellectuals in China can play a vanguard role or serve as a link with the masses, not all of them will remain revolutionaries to the end. Some will drop out of the revolutionary ranks at critical moments and become passive, while a few may even become enemies of the revolution. The intellectuals can overcome their shortcomings only in mass struggles over a long period.

Second, are the small tradesmen. Generally they run small shops and employ few or no assistants. They live under the threat of bankruptcy as a result of exploitation by imperialism, the big bourgeoisie and the usurers.

Third, the handicraftsmen. They are very numerous. They possess their own means of production and hire no workers, or only one or two apprentices or helpers. Their position is similar to that of the middle peasants.

Fourth, professional people. They include doctors and men of other professions. They do not exploit other people, or do so only to a slight degree. Their position is similar to that of the handicraftsmen.

These sections of the petty bourgeoisie make up a vast multitude of people whom we must win over and whose interests we must protect because in general they can support or join the revolution and are good allies. Their weakness is that some of them are easily influenced by the bourgeoisie; consequently, we must carry on revolutionary propaganda and organizational work among them.

4. The Peasantry

The peasantry constitutes approximately 80 per cent of China's total population and is the main force in her national economy today.

A sharp process of polarization is taking place among the peasantry.

First, the rich peasants. They form about 5 per cent of the rural population (or about 10 per cent together with the landlords) and constitute the rural bourgeoisie. Most of the rich peasants in China are semi-feudal in character, since they let a part of their land, practice usury and ruthlessly exploit the farm laborers. But they generally engage in labor themselves and in this sense are part of the peasantry. The rich-peasant form of production will remain useful for a definite period. Generally speaking, they might make some contribution to the anti-imperialist struggle of the peasant masses and stay neutral in the agrarian revolutionary struggle against the landlords. Therefore we should not regard the rich peasants as belonging to the same class as the landlords and should not prematurely adopt a policy of liquidating the rich peasantry.

Second, the middle peasants. They form about 20 per cent of China's rural population. They are economically self-supporting (they may have something to lay aside when the crops are good, and occasionally hire some labor or lend small sums of money at interest); and generally they do not exploit others but are exploited by imperialism, the landlord class and the bourgeoisie. They have no political rights. Some of them do not have enough land, and only a section (the well-to-do middle peasants) have some surplus land. Not only can the middle peasants join the anti-imperialist revolution and the Agrarian Revolution, but they can also accept socialism. Therefore the whole middle peasantry can be a reliable ally of the proletariat and is an important motive force of the revolution. The positive or negative attitude of the middle peasants is one of the factors determining victory or defeat in the revolution, and this is especially true after the agrarian revolution when they become the majority of the rural population.

Third, the poor peasants. The poor peasants in China, together with the farm laborers, form about 70 per cent of the rural population. They are the broad peasant masses with no land or insufficient land, the semi-proletariat of the countryside, the biggest motive force of the Chinese revolution, the natural and most reliable ally of the proletariat and the main contingent of China's revolutionary forces. Only under the leadership of the proletariat can the poor and middle peasants achieve their liberation, and only by forming a firm alliance with the poor and middle peasants can the proletariat lead the revolution to victory. Otherwise neither is possible. The term "peasantry" refers mainly to the poor and middle peasants.

5. The Proletariat

Among the Chinese proletariat, the modern industrial workers number from 2,500,000 to 3,000,000, the workers in small-scale industry and in handicrafts and the shop assistants in the cities total about 12,000,000, and in addition there are great numbers of rural proletarians (the farm laborers) and other propertyless people in the cities and the countryside.

In addition to the basic qualities it shares with the proletariat everywhere--its association with the most advanced form of economy, its strong sense of organization and discipline and its lack of private means of production--the Chinese proletariat has many other outstanding qualities.

What are they?

First, the Chinese proletariat is more resolute and thoroughgoing in revolutionary struggle than any other class because it is subjected to a threefold oppression (imperialist, bourgeois and feudal) which is marked by a severity and cruelty seldom found in other countries. Since there is no economic basis for social reformism in colonial and semi-colonial China as there is in Europe, the whole proletariat, with the exception of a few scabs, is most revolutionary.

Secondly, from the moment it appeared on the revolutionary scene, the Chinese proletariat came under the leadership of its own revolutionary party--the Communist Party of China--and became the most politically conscious class in Chinese society.

Thirdly, because the Chinese proletariat by origin is largely made up of bankrupted peasants, it has natural ties with the peasant masses, which facilitates its forming a close alliance with them.

Therefore, in spite of certain unavoidable weaknesses, for instance, its smallness (as compared with the peasantry), its youth (as compared with the proletariat in the capitalist countries) and its low educational level (as compared with the bourgeoisie), the Chinese proletariat is nonetheless the basic motive force of the Chinese revolution. Unless it is led by the proletariat, the Chinese revolution cannot possibly succeed. To take an example from the past, the Revolution of 1911 miscarried because the proletariat did not consciously participate in it and the Communist Party was not yet in existence. More recently, the revolution of 1924-27 achieved great success for a time because the proletariat consciously participated and exercised leadership and the Communist Party was already in existence; it ended in defeat because the big bourgeoisie betrayed its alliance with the proletariat and abandoned the common revolutionary program, and also because the Chinese proletariat and its political party did not yet have enough revolutionary experience. Now take the present anti-Japanese war--because the proletariat and the Communist Party are exercising leadership in the Anti-Japanese National United Front, the whole nation has been united and the great War of Resistance has been launched and is being resolutely pursued.

The Chinese proletariat should understand that although it is the class with the highest political consciousness and sense of organization, it cannot win victory by its own strength alone. In order to win, it must unite, according to varying circumstances, with all classes and strata that can take part in the revolution, and must organize a revolutionary united front. Among all the classes in Chinese society, the peasantry is a firm ally of the working class, the urban petty bourgeoisie is a reliable ally, and the national bourgeoisie is an ally in certain periods and to a certain extent. This is one of the fundamental laws established by China's modern revolutionary history.

6. The Vagrants

China's status as a colony and semi-colony has given rise to a multitude of rural and urban unemployed. Denied proper means of making a living, many of them are forced to resort to illegitimate ones, hence the robbers, gangsters, beggars and prostitutes and the numerous people who live on superstitious practices. This social stratum is unstable; while some are apt to be bought over by the reactionary forces, others may join the revolution. These people lack constructive qualities and are given to destruction rather than construction; after joining the revolution, they become a source of roving-rebel and anarchist ideology in the revolutionary ranks. Therefore, we should know how to re-mould them and guard against their destructiveness.

The above is our analysis of the motive forces of the Chinese revolution.

THE CHARACTER OF THE CHINESE REVOLUTION

We have now gained an understanding of the nature of Chinese society, *i.e.,* of the specific conditions in China; this understanding is the essential prerequisite for solving all China's revolutionary problems. We are also clear about the targets, the tasks and the motive forces of the Chinese revolution; these are basic issues at the present stage of the revolution and arise from the special nature of Chinese society, *i.e.,* from China's specific conditions. Understanding all this, we can now understand another basic issue of the revolution at the present stage, *i.e.,* the character of the Chinese revolution.

What, indeed, is the character of the Chinese revolution at the present stage? Is it a bourgeois-democratic or a proletarian-socialist revolution? Obviously, it is not the latter but the former.

Since Chinese society is colonial, semi-colonial and semi-feudal, since the principal enemies of the Chinese revolution are imperialism and feudalism, since the tasks of the revolution are to overthrow these two enemies by means of a national and democratic revolution in which the bourgeoisie sometimes takes part, and since the edge of the revolution is directed against imperialism and feudalism and not against capitalism and capitalist private property in general even if the big bourgeoisie betrays the revolution and becomes its enemy -- since all this is true, the character of the Chinese revolution at the present stage is not proletarian-socialist but bourgeois-democratic. [23]

However, in present-day China the bourgeois-democratic revolution is no longer of the old general type, which is now obsolete, but one of a new special type. We call this type the new-democratic revolution and it is developing in all other colonial and semi-colonial countries as well as in China. The new-democratic revolution is part of the world proletarian-socialist revolution, for it resolutely opposes imperialism, *i.e.,* international capitalism. Politically, it strives for the joint dictatorship of the revolutionary classes over the imperialists, traitors and reactionaries, and opposes the transformation of Chinese society into a society under bourgeois dictatorship. Economically, it aims at the nationalization of all the big enterprises and capital of the imperialists, traitors and reactionaries, and the distribution among the peasants of the land held by the landlords, while preserving private capitalist enterprise in general and not eliminating the rich-peasant economy. Thus, the new type of democratic revolution clears the way for capitalism on the one hand and creates the prerequisites for socialism on the other. The present stage of the Chinese revolution is a stage of transition between the abolition of the colonial, semi-colonial and semi-feudal society and the establishment of a socialist society, *i.e.,* it is a process of new-democratic revolution. This process, begun only after the First World War and the Russian October Revolution, started in China with the May 4th Movement of 1919. A new-democratic revolution is an anti-imperialist and anti-feudal revolution of the broad masses of the people under the leadership of the proletariat. Chinese society can advance to socialism only through such a revolution; there is no other way.

The new-democratic revolution is vastly different from the democratic revolutions of Europe and America in that it results not in a dictatorship of the bourgeoisie but in a dictatorship of the united front of all the revolutionary classes under the leadership of the proletariat. In the present War of Resistance, the anti-Japanese democratic political power established in the base areas which are under the leadership of the Communist Party is the political power of the Anti-Japanese National United Front; this is neither a bourgeois nor a proletarian one-class dictatorship, but a joint dictatorship of the revolutionary classes under the leadership of the proletariat. All who stand for resistance to Japan and for democracy are entitled to share in this political power, regardless of their party affiliation.

The new-democratic revolution also differs from a socialist revolution in that it overthrows the rule of the imperialists, traitors and reactionaries in China but does not destroy any section of capitalism which is capable of contributing to the anti-imperialist, anti-feudal struggle.

The new-democratic revolution is basically in line with the revolution envisaged in the Three People's Principles as advocated by Dr. Sun Yat-sen in 1924. In the Manifesto of the First National Congress of the Kuomintang issued in that year, Dr. Sun stated:

The so-called democratic system in modern states is usually monopolized by the bourgeoisie and has become simply an instrument for oppressing the common people. On the other hand the Kuomintang's Principle of Democracy means a democratic system shared by all the common people and not privately owned by the few.

He added:

Enterprises, such as banks, railways and airlines, whether Chinese-owned or foreign-owned, which are either monopolistic in character or too big for private management, shall be operated and administrated by the state, so that private capital cannot dominate the livelihood of the people: this is the main principle of the regulation of capital.

And again in his Testament, Dr. Sun pointed out the fundamental principle for domestic and foreign policy: "We must arouse the masses of the people and unite in a common struggle with those nations of the world which treat us as equals." The Three People's Principles of the old democracy, which were adapted to the old international and domestic conditions, were thus reshaped into the Three People's Principles of New Democracy, which are adapted to the new international and domestic conditions. The Communist Party of China was referring to the latter kind of Three People's Principles and to no other when, in its Manifesto of September 22, 1937, it declared that "the Three People's Principles being what China needs today, our Party is ready to fight for their complete realization". These Three People's Principles embody Dr. Sun Yat-sen's Three Great Policies--alliance with Russia, co-operation with the Communist Party and assistance to the peasants and workers. In the new international and domestic conditions, any kind of Three People's Principles which departs from the Three Great Policies is not revolutionary. (Here we shall not deal with the fact that, while communism and the Three People's Principles agree on the basic political program for the democratic revolution, they differ in all other respects.)

Thus, the role of the proletariat, the peasantry and the other sections of the petty bourgeoisie in China's bourgeois-democratic revolution cannot be ignored, either in the alignment of forces for the struggle (that is, in the united front) or in the organization of state power. Anyone who tries to bypass these classes will certainly be unable to solve the problem of the destiny of the Chinese nation or indeed any of China's problems. The Chinese revolution at the present stage must strive to create a democratic republic in which the workers, the peasants and the other sections of the petty bourgeoisie all occupy a definite position and play a definite role. In other words, it must be a democratic republic based on a revolutionary alliance of the workers' peasants, urban petty bourgeoisie and all others who are against imperialism and feudalism. Only under the leadership of the proletariat can such a republic be completely realized.

THE PERSPECTIVES OF THE CHINESE REVOLUTION

Now that the basic issues--the nature of Chinese society and the targets, tasks, motive forces and character of the Chinese revolution at the present stage--have been clarified, it is easy to see its perspectives, that is, to understand the relation between the bourgeois-democratic and the proletarian-socialist revolution, or between the present and future stages of the Chinese revolution.

There can be no doubt that the ultimate perspective of the Chinese revolution is not capitalism but socialism and communism, since China's bourgeois-democratic revolution at the present stage is not of the old general type but is a democratic revolution of a new special type-- a new-democratic revolution--and since it is taking place in the new international environment of the Nineteen Thirties and Forties characterized by the rise of socialism and the decline of capitalism, in the period of the Second World War and the era of revolution.

However, it is not at all surprising but entirely to be expected that a capitalist economy will develop to a certain extent within Chinese society with the sweeping away of the obstacles to the development of capitalism after the victory of the revolution, since the purpose of the Chinese revolution at the present stage is to change the existing colonial, semi-colonial and semi-feudal state of society, *i.e.*, to strive for the completion of the new-democratic revolution. A certain degree of capitalist development will be an inevitable result of the victory of the democratic revolution in economically backward China. But that will be only one aspect of the outcome of the Chinese revolution and not the whole picture. The whole picture will show the development of socialist as well as capitalist factors. What will the socialist factors be? The increasing relative importance of the proletariat and the Communist Party among the political forces in the country; leadership by the proletariat and the Communist Party which the peasantry, intelligentsia and the urban petty bourgeoisie already accept or are likely to accept; and the state sector of the economy owned by the democratic republic, and the co-operative sector of the economy owned by the working people. All these will be socialist factors. With the addition of a favorable international environment, these factors render it highly probable that China's bourgeois-democratic revolution will ultimately avoid a capitalist future and enjoy a socialist future.

THE TWOFOLD TASK OF THE CHINESE REVOLUTION AND THE CHINESE COMMUNIST PARTY

Summing up the foregoing sections of this chapter, we can see that the Chinese revolution taken as a whole involves a twofold task. That is to say, it embraces both the bourgeois-democratic revolution (the new-democratic revolution) and the proletarian-socialist revolution, *i.e.,* both the present and future stages of the revolution. The leadership in this twofold revolutionary task devolves on the Chinese Communist Party, the party of the proletariat, without whose leadership no revolution can succeed.

To complete China's bourgeois-democratic revolution (the new-democratic revolution) and to transform it into a socialist revolution when all the necessary conditions are ripe--such is the sum total of the great and glorious revolutionary task of the Chinese Communist Party. Every Party member must strive for its accomplishment and must under no circumstances give up halfway. Some immature Communists think that our task is confined to the present democratic revolution and does not include the future socialist revolution, or that the present revolution or the Agrarian Revolution is actually a socialist revolution. It must be emphatically pointed out that these views are wrong. Every Communist ought to know that, taken as a whole, the Chinese revolutionary movement led by the Communist Party embraces the two stages, *i.e.,* the democratic and the socialist revolutions, which are two essentially different revolutionary processes, and that the second process can be carried through only after the first has been completed.

The democratic revolution is the necessary preparation for the socialist revolution, and the socialist revolution is the inevitable sequel to the democratic revolution. The ultimate aim for which all communists strive is to bring about a socialist and communist society. A clear understanding of both the differences and the interconnections between the democratic and the socialist revolutions is indispensable to correct leadership in the Chinese revolution.

Except for the Communist Party, no political party (bourgeois or petty-bourgeois) is equal to the task of leading China's two great revolutions, the democratic and the socialist revolutions, to complete fulfillment. From the very day of its birth, the Communist Party has taken this twofold task on its own shoulders and for eighteen years has fought strenuously for its accomplishment.

It is a task at once glorious and arduous. And it cannot be accomplished without a bolshevized Chinese Communist Party which is national in scale and has a broad mass character, a party fully consolidated ideologically, politically and organizationally. Therefore every Communist has the duty of playing an active part in building up such a Communist Party.

NOTES

1. With reference to the invention of the compass, the magnetic power of the loadstone was mentioned as early as the 3rd century BC by Lu Pu-wei in his *Almanac,* and at the beginning of the 1st century AD, Wang Chung, the materialist philosopher, observed in his *Lun Heng* that the loadstone points to the south, which indicates that magnetic polarity was known by then. Works of travel written at the beginning of the 12th century show that the compass was already in general use among Chinese navigators at that time.

2. It is recorded in ancient documents that Tsai Lun, a eunuch of the Eastern Han Dynasty (AD 25-220), invented paper, which he had made from bark, hemp, rags and worn-out fishing nets. In AD 105 (the last year of the reign of Emperor Ho Ti), Tsai Lun presented his invention to the emperor, and subsequently this method of making paper from plant fiber gradually spread in China.

3. Block-printing was invented about A.D. 600, in the Sui Dynasty.

4. Movable type was invented by Pi Sheng in the Sung Dynasty between 1041 and 1048.

5. According to tradition, gunpowder was invented in China in the 9th century and by the 11th century it was already in use for firing cannon.

6. Chen Sheng, Wu Kuang, Hsian Yu and Liu Pang were leaders of the first great peasant uprising in the Chin Dynasty. In 209 B.C. Chen Sheng and Wu Kuang, who were among nine hundred conscripts on their way to take up garrison duty at a frontier post, organized a revolt in Chihsien County (now

Suhsien County in Anhwei Province) against the tyranny of the Chin Dynasty. Hsiang Yu and Liu Pang were the most prominent of those who rose in response to this armed uprising all over the country. Hsiang Yu's army annihilated the main forces of Chin, and Liu Pang's troops took Chin's capital. In the ensuing struggle between Liu Pang and Hsiang Yu, Liu Pang defeated Hsiang Yu and founded the Han Dynasty.

7. The Hsinshih, the Pinglin, the Red Eyebrows and the Bronze Horses are the names of peasant uprisings in the latter years of the Western Han Dynasty when peasant unrest was widespread. In A.D. 8, Wang Mang overthrew the reigning dynasty, ascended the throne and introduced a few reforms to stave off the peasant unrest. But the starving masses in Hsinshih (in what is now Chingshan County in Hupeh) and Pinglin (in what is now Suihsien County in Hupeh) rose in revolt. The Bronze Horses and the Red Eyebrows were the peasant forces which revolted during his reign in what are now central Hopei and central Shantung Provinces. The Red Eyebrows, the largest of the peasant forces, were so named because the soldiers painted their eyebrows red.

8. The Yellow Turbans, a peasant force which revolted in A.D. 184, were named after their headgear.

9. Li Mi and Tou Chien-teh were leaders of great peasant uprisings against the Sui Dynasty in Honan and Hopei respectively at the opening of the 7th century.

10. Wang Hsien-chih organized an uprising in Shantung in A.D. 874. In the following year Huang Chao organized an uprising to support him.

11. Sung Chiang and Fang La were famous leaders of peasant uprisings early in the 12th century; Sung Chiang was active

along the borders between Shantung, Hopei, Honan and Kiangsu, while Fang La was active in Chekiang and Anhwei.

12. In 1351, the people in many parts of the country rose in revolt against the rule of the Yuan (Mongol) Dynasty. In 1352, Chu Yuan-chang joined the rebel forces led by Kuo Tzu-hsing and became their commander upon the latter's death. In 1368, he finally succeeded in overthrowing the rule of the Mongol Dynasty, which had been tottering under the attacks of the people's forces, and founded the Ming Dynasty.

13. Li Tzu-cheng, also called King Chuang (the Dare-All King), native of Michih, northern Shensi, was the leader of a peasant revolt which led to the overthrow of the Ming Dynasty. The revolt first started in northern Shensi in 1628. Li joined the forces led by Kao Ying-hsiang and campaigned through Honan and Anhwei and back to Shensi. After Kao's death in 1636, Li succeeded him, becoming King Chuang, and campaigned in and out of the provinces of Shensi, Szechuan, Honan and Hupeh. Finally he captured the imperial capital of Peking in 1644, whereupon the last Ming emperor committed suicide. The chief slogan he spread among the masses was "Support King Chuang, and pay no grain taxes". Another slogan of his to enforce discipline among his men ran: "Any murder means the killing of my father, any rape means the violation of my mother." Thus he won the support of the masses and his movement became the main current of the peasant revolts raging all over the country. As he, too, roamed about without ever establishing relatively consolidated base areas, he was eventually defeated by Wu San-kuei, a Ming general, who colluded with the Ching troops in a joint attack on Li.

14. From 1856 to 1860 Britain and France jointly waged a war of aggression against China, with the United States and tsarist Russia supporting them from the side-lines. The government of

the Ching Dynasty was then devoting all its energies to suppressing the peasant revolution of the Taiping Heavenly Kingdom and adopted a policy of passive resistance towards the foreign aggressors. The Anglo-French forces occupied such major cities as Canton, Tientsin and Peking, plundered and burned down the Yuan Ming Yuan Palace in Peking and forced the Ching government to conclude the Treaties of Tientsin and Peking. Their main provisions included the opening of Tientsin, Newchwang, Tengchow, Taiwan, Tamsui, Chaochow, Chiungchow, Nanking, Chinkiang, Kinkiang and Hankow as treaty ports, and the granting to foreigners of special privileges for travel, missionary activities and inland navigation in China's interior. From then on, the foreign forces of aggression spread through all China's coastal provinces and penetrated deep into the hinterland.

15. In 1882-83, the French aggressors invaded the northern part of Indo-China. In 1884-85 they extended their war of aggression to the Chinese provinces of Kwangsi, Taiwan, Fukien and Chekiang. Despite the victories gained in this war, the corrupt Ching government signed the humiliating Treaty of Tientsin.

16. In 1900 eight imperialist powers, Britain, the United States, Germany, France, tsarist Russia, Japan, Italy and Austria, sent a joint force to attack China in their attempt to suppress the Yi Ho Tuan Movement of the Chinese people against aggression. The Chinese people resisted heroically. The allied forces of the eight powers captured Taku and occupied Tientsin and Peking. In 1901 the Ching government concluded a treaty with the eight imperialist countries; its main provisions were that China had to pay those countries the huge sum of 450 million taels of silver as war reparations and grant them the special privilege of stationing troops in Peking and in the area from Peking to Tientsin and Shanhaikuan.

17. Consular jurisdiction was one of the special privileges provided in the unequal treaties which the imperialist powers forced on the governments of old China-- beginning with the supplementary treaty to the Sino-British Treaty of Nanking, signed at Humen (the Bogue) in 1843, and with the Sino-American Treaty of Wanghia in 1844. It meant that, if a national of any country enjoying the privilege of consular jurisdiction in China became a defendant in a lawsuit, civil or criminal, he was not to be tried by a Chinese court but by the consul of his own country.

18. Spheres of influence were different parts of China marked off at the end of the 19th century by the imperialist powers that committed aggression against China. Each of these powers marked off those areas which fell within its economic and military influence. Thus, the provinces in the lower and middle Yangtse valley were specified as the British sphere of influence; Yunnan, Kwangtung and Kwangsi as the French; Shantung as the German sphere; Fukien as the Japanese, and the three northeastern provinces (the present provinces of Liaoning, Kirin and Heilungkiang) as the tsarist Russian sphere. After the Russo-Japanese War of 1905 the southern part of the three northeastern provinces came under Japanese influence.

19. The foreign concessions were areas which the imperialist powers seized in the treaty ports after compelling the Ching government to open these ports. In these so-called concessions they enforced an imperialist system of colonial rule entirely independent of Chinese law and administration. Through those concessions, the imperialists exercised direct or indirect political and economic control over the Chinese feudal and comprador regime. During the revolution of 1924-27 the revolutionary people led by the Chinese Communist Party started a movement to abolish the concessions, and in January

1927 they took over the British concessions in Hankow and Kiukiang. However, the imperialists retained various concessions after Chiang Kai-shek betrayed the revolution.

20. "The Theses on the Revolutionary Movement in Colonial and Semi-Colonial Countries" adopted by the Sixth Comintern Congress, stenographic record of the Sixth Comintern Congress, issue No. 6, Russ. ed., Moscow, 1929, p. 128.

21. J. V. Stalin, "The Revolution in China and the Tasks of the Comintern", *Works*, Eng. ed., FLPH, Moscow, 1954, Vol. IX, p. 292.

22. J. V. Stalin, "The Prospects of the Revolution in China", Works, Eng. ed. FLPH, Moscow, 1954, Vol. VIII, p. 379.

23. See V. I. Lenin, "The Agrarian Program of Social-Democracy in the First Russian Revolution, 1905-1907", *Collected Works,* Eng. ed., FLPH, Moscow, 1962, Vol. XIII, pp. 219-429.

COLLECTED WRITINGS
OF
CHAIRMAN MAO

POLITICS AND TACTICS

PART 4

THE ROLE OF
THE CHINESE
COMMUNIST PARTY
IN THE NATIONAL WAR

Mao Zedong

Preface

October 1938

This report was made by Comrade Mao Zedong to the Sixth Plenary Session of the Sixth Central Committee of the Party. In discussing the question of the role of the Chinese Communist Party in the national war he helped all comrades clearly to understand and conscientiously to shoulder the Party's great and historic responsibility of leading the War of Resistance against Japan.

The plenary session decided on the line of persisting in the anti-Japanese united front, but at the same time pointed out that there had to be struggle as well as unity within the united front and that the proposition, "Everything through the united front", did not suit Chinese conditions. Thus the error of accommodationism in regard to the united front was criticized; this problem was dealt with by Comrade Mao Zedong in "The Question of Independence and Initiative within the United Front", which was part of his concluding speech at the same session.

Comrades, the prospects ahead of us are bright. Not only is it necessary for us to defeat Japanese imperialism and build a new China, but we are certainly capable of achieving these aims. However, there is a difficult road ahead between the present and the bright future. In the struggle for a new China, the Chinese Communist Party and the whole people must fight the Japanese aggressors in a planned way and can defeat them only through a long war. We have already said a good deal about the various problems relating to the war. We have summed up the experience gained since its outbreak and appraised the present situation, defined the urgent tasks confronting the whole nation and explained the reasons for sustaining a long war by means of a long-term national united front against Japan and the methods for doing so, and we have analyzed the international situation. What problems then remain? Comrades, there is one more problem, namely, what role the Chinese Communist Party should play in the national war, or how Communists should understand their own role, strengthen themselves and close their ranks in order to be able to lead this war to victory and not to defeat.

PATRIOTISM AND INTERNATIONALISM

Can a Communist, who is an internationalist, at the same time be a patriot? We hold that he not only can be but must be. The specific content of patriotism is determined by historical conditions. There is the "patriotism" of the Japanese aggressors and of Hitler, and there is our patriotism. Communists must resolutely oppose the "patriotism" of the Japanese aggressors and of Hitler. The Communists of Japan and Germany are defeatists with regard to the wars being waged by their countries. To bring about the defeat of the Japanese aggressors and of Hitler by every possible means is in the interests of the Japanese and the German people, and the more complete the defeat the better. This is what the Japanese and German

Communists should be doing and what they are doing. For the wars launched by the Japanese aggressors and Hitler are harming their own people as well as the people of the world. China's case is different, because she is the victim of aggression. Chinese Communists must therefore combine patriotism with internationalism. We are at once internationalists and patriots, and our slogan is, "Fight to defend the motherland against the aggressors." For us defeatism is a crime and to strive for victory in the War of Resistance is an inescapable duty. For only by fighting in defense of the motherland can we defeat the aggressors and achieve national liberation. And only by achieving national liberation will it be possible for the proletariat and other working people to achieve their own emancipation. The victory of China and the defeat of the invading imperialists will help the people of other countries. Thus in wars of national liberation, patriotism is applied to internationalism. For this reason Communists must use their initiative to the full, march bravely and resolutely to the battle front of the war of national liberation and train their guns on the Japanese aggressors. For this reason, immediately after the Incident of September 18, 1931, our Party issued its call to resist the Japanese aggressors by a war of national defense, and later proposed a national united front against Japan, ordered the Red Army to reorganize as part of the anti-Japanese National Revolutionary Army and to march to the front, and instructed Party members to take their place in the forefront of the war and defend the motherland to the last drop of their blood. These are good patriotic actions and, far from running counter to internationalism, are its application in China. Only those who are politically muddle-headed or have ulterior motives talk nonsense about our having made a mistake and abandoned internationalism.

COMMUNISTS SHOULD SET AN EXAMPLE IN THE
NATIONAL WAR

For the above reasons Communists should show a high degree
of initiative in the national war, and show it concretely, that is,
they should play an exemplary vanguard role in every sphere.
Our war is being waged under adverse circumstances. National
consciousness, national self-respect and national self-
confidence are not sufficiently developed among the broad
masses, the majority of the people are unorganized, China's
military power is weak, the economy is backward, the political
system is undemocratic, corruption and pessimism exist, and a
lack of unity and solidarity is to be found within the united
front; these are among the adverse circumstances. Therefore,
Communists must consciously shoulder the great responsibility
of uniting the entire nation so as to put an end to all such
undesirable phenomena. Here the exemplary vanguard role of
the Communists is of vital importance. Communists in the
Eighth Route and New Fourth Armies should set an example in
fighting bravely, carrying out orders, observing discipline,
doing political work and fostering internal unity and solidarity.
In their relations with friendly parties and armies, Communists
should take a firm stand of unity for resistance to Japan, uphold
the program of the united front and set an example in carrying
out the tasks of resistance; they should be true in word and
resolute indeed, free from arrogance and sincere in consulting
and co-operating with the friendly parties and armies, and they
should be models in inter-party relations within the united
front. Every Communist engaged in government work should
set an example of absolute integrity, of freedom from
favoritism in making appointments and of hard work for little
remuneration. Every Communist working among the masses
should be their friend and not a boss over them, an
indefatigable teacher and not a bureaucratic politician. At no
time and in no circumstances should a Communist place his

personal interests first; he should subordinate them to the interests of the nation and of the masses. Hence, selfishness, slacking, corruption, seeking the limelight, and so on, are most contemptible, while selflessness, working with all one's energy, whole-hearted devotion to public duty, and quiet hard work will command respect. Communists should work in harmony with all progressives outside the Party and endeavor to unite the entire people to do away with whatever is undesirable. It must be realized that Communists form only a small section of the nation, and that there are large numbers of progressives and activists outside the Party with whom we must work. It is entirely wrong to think that we alone are good and no one else is any good. As for people who are politically backward, Communists should not slight or despise them, but should befriend them, unite with them, convince them and encourage them to go forward. The attitude of Communists towards any person who has made mistakes in his work should be one of persuasion in order to help him change and start afresh and not one of exclusion, unless he is incorrigible. Communists should set an example in being practical as well as far-sighted. For only by being practical can they fulfill the appointed tasks, and only far-sightedness can prevent them from losing their bearings in the march forward. Communists should therefore set an example in study; at all times they should learn from the masses as well as teach them. Only by learning from the people, from actual circumstances and from the friendly parties and armies, and by knowing them well, can we be practical in our work and far-sighted as to the future. In a long war and in adverse circumstances, the dynamic energy of the whole nation can be mobilized in the struggle to overcome difficulties, defeat the enemy and build a new China only if the Communists play an exemplary vanguard role to the best of their ability together with all the advanced elements among the friendly parties and armies and among the masses.

UNITE THE WHOLE NATION AND COMBAT ENEMY AGENTS IN ITS MIDST

The one and only policy for overcoming difficulties, defeating the enemy and building a new China is to consolidate and expand the Anti-Japanese National United Front and mobilize the dynamic energy of the whole nation. However, there are already enemy agents playing a disruptive role within our national united front, namely, the traitors, Trotskyites and pro-Japanese elements. Communists must always be on the look-out for them, expose their criminal activities with factual evidence and warn the people not to be duped by them. Communists must sharpen their political vigilance towards these enemy agents. They must understand that the expansion and consolidation of the national united front is inseparable from the exposure and weeding out of enemy agents. It is entirely wrong to pay attention only to the one side and forget the other.

EXPAND THE COMMUNIST PARTY AND PREVENT INFILTRATION BY ENEMY AGENTS

To overcome the difficulties, defeat the enemy and build a new China, the Communist Party must expand its organization and become a great mass party by opening its doors to the masses of workers, peasants and young activists who are truly devoted to the revolution, who believe in the Party's principles, support its policies and are willing to observe its discipline and work hard. Here no tendency towards closed-doorism should be tolerated. But at the same time, there must be no slackening of vigilance against infiltration by enemy agents. The Japanese imperialist secret services are ceaselessly trying to disrupt our Party and to smuggle undercover traitors, Trotskyites, pro-Japanese elements, degenerates and careerists into its ranks in the guise of activists. Not for a moment must we relax our vigilance and our strict precautions against such persons. We must not close our doors for fear of enemy agents, our set policy being boldly to expand our Party. But while boldly enlarging our membership, we must not relax our vigilance against enemy agents and careerists who will avail themselves of this opportunity to sneak in. We shall make mistakes if we only pay attention to the one side and forget the other. The only correct policy is: "Expand the Party boldly but do not let a single undesirable in."

MAINTAIN BOTH THE UNITED FRONT AND THE INDEPENDENCE OF THE PARTY

It is only by firmly maintaining the national united front that the difficulties can be overcome, the enemy defeated and a new China built. This is beyond all doubt. At the same time, every party and group in the united front must preserve its ideological, political and organizational independence; this holds good for the Kuomintang, the Communist Party or any other party or group. In inter-party relations, the Principle of Democracy in the Three People's Principles permits both the union of all parties and groups and the independent existence of each. To speak of unity alone while-denying independence is to abandon the Principle of Democracy, and to this neither the Communist Party nor any other party would agree. There is no doubt that independence within the united front is relative and not absolute, and that to regard it as absolute would undermine the general policy of unity against the enemy. But this relative independence must not be denied; ideologically, politically and organizationally, each party must have its relative independence, that is, relative freedom. Also, the general policy of unity against the enemy would be undermined if this relative freedom were denied or voluntarily abandoned. This should be clearly understood by all members of the Communist Party as well as of the friendly parties.

The same is true of the relationship between the class struggle and the national struggle. It is an established principle that in the War of Resistance everything must be subordinated to the interests of resistance. Therefore, the interests of the class struggle must be subordinated to, and must not conflict with, the interests of the War of Resistance. But classes and the class struggle are facts, and those people who deny the fact of class struggle are wrong. The theory which attempts to deny this fact is utterly wrong. We do not deny the class struggle, we adjust it. The policy of mutual help and mutual concessions which we advocate is applicable not only to party relations but also to class relations. Unity against Japan requires an appropriate policy of adjustment in class relations, a policy which does not leave the laboring people without political and material safeguards but also gives consideration to the interests of the rich, thereby meeting the demands of solidarity against the enemy. It is bad for the War of Resistance to pay attention only to the one side and neglect the other.

CONSIDER THE SITUATION AS A WHOLE, THINK IN TERMS OF THE MAJORITY, AND WORK TOGETHER WITH OUR ALLIES

In leading the masses in struggle against the enemy, Communists must consider the situation as a whole, think in terms of the majority of the people and work together with their allies. They must grasp the principle of subordinating the needs of the part to the needs of the whole. If a proposal appears feasible for a partial situation but not for the situation as a whole, then the part must give way to the whole. Conversely, if the proposal is not feasible for the part but is feasible in the light of the situation as a whole, again the part must give way to the whole. This is what is meant by considering the situation as a whole. Communists must never separate themselves from the majority of the people or neglect them by leading only a few progressive contingents in an isolated and rash advance, but must forge close links between the progressive elements and the broad masses. This is what is meant by thinking in terms of the majority. Wherever there are democratic parties or individuals willing to co-operate with us, the proper attitude for Communists is to talk things over with them and work together with them. It is wrong to indulge in arbitrary decisions and peremptory actions and to ignore our allies. A good Communist must be good at considering the situation as a whole, good at thinking in terms of the majority and good at working with his allies. We have had serious shortcomings in this respect, and we must still give the matter attention.

CADRES POLICY

The Chinese Communist Party is a party leading a great revolutionary struggle in a nation several hundred million strong, and it cannot fulfill its historic task without a large number of leading cadres who combine ability with political integrity. In the last seventeen years our Party has trained a good many competent leaders, so that we have a framework of cadres in military, political, cultural, Party and mass work; all honor is due to the Party and to the nation for this achievement. But the present framework is not yet strong enough to support the vast edifice of our struggle, and it is still necessary to train capable people on a large scale. Many activists have come forward, and are continuing to come forward, in the great struggle of the Chinese people. We have the responsibility for organizing and training them and for taking good care and making proper use of them. Cadres are a decisive factor, once the political line is determined. [1] Therefore, it is our fighting task to train large numbers of new cadres in a planned way.

Our concern should extend to non-Party cadres as well as to Party cadres. There are many capable people outside the Party whom we must not ignore. The duty of every Communist is to rid himself of aloofness and arrogance and to work well with non-Party cadres, give them sincere help, have a warm, comradely attitude towards them and enlist their initiative in the great cause of resisting Japan and reconstructing the nation.

We must know how to judge cadres. We must not confine our judgment to a short period or a single incident in a cadre's life, but should consider his life and work as a whole. This is the principal method of judging cadres.

We must know how to use cadres well. In the final analysis, leadership involves two main responsibilities: to work out ideas, and to use cadres well. Such things as drawing up plans, making decisions, and giving orders and directives, are all in the category of "working out ideas". To put the ideas into practice, we must weld the cadres together and encourage them to go into action; this comes into the category of "using the cadres well". Throughout our national history there have been two sharply contrasting lines on the subject of the use of cadres, one being to "appoint people on their merit", and the other to "appoint people by favoritism". The former is the honest and the latter the dishonest way. The criterion the Communist Party should apply in its cadres policy is whether or not a cadre is resolute in carrying out the Party line, keeps to Party discipline, has close ties with the masses, has the ability to find his bearings independently, and is active, hard-working and unselfish. This is what "appointing people on their merit" means. The cadres policy of Chang Kuo-tao was the exact opposite. Following the line of "appointing people by favoritism," he gathered personal favorites round himself to form a small clique, and in the end he turned traitor to the Party and decamped. This is an important lesson for us. Taking

Mao Zedong

warning from it and from similar historical lessons, the Central Committee and the leaders at all levels must make it their major responsibility to adhere to the honest and fair way in cadres policy and reject the dishonest and unfair way, and so consolidate the unity of the Party.

We must know how to take good care of cadres. There are several ways of doing so.

First, give them guidance. This means allowing them a free hand in their work so that they have the courage to assume responsibility and, at the same time, giving them timely instructions so that, guided by the Party's political line, they are able to make full use of their initiative.

Second, raise their level. This means educating them by giving them the opportunity to study so that they can enhance their theoretical understanding and their working ability.

Third, check up on their work, and help them sum up their experience, carry forward their achievements and correct their mistakes. To assign work without checking up and to take notice only when serious mistakes are made--that is not the way to take care of cadres.

Fourth, in general, use the method of persuasion with cadres who have made mistakes, and help them correct their mistakes. The method of struggle should be confined to those who make serious mistakes and nevertheless refuse to accept guidance. Here patience is essential. It is wrong lightly to label people "opportunists" or lightly to begin "waging struggles" against them.

Fifth, help them with their difficulties. When cadres in difficulty as a result of illness, straitened means or domestic or other troubles, we must be sure to give them as much care as possible.

This is how to take good care of cadres.

PARTY DISCIPLINE

In view of Chang Kuo-tao's serious violations of discipline, we must affirm anew the discipline of the Party, namely:

(1) the individual is subordinate to the organization;

(2) the minority is subordinate to the majority;

(3) the lower level is subordinate to the higher level; and

(4) the entire membership is subordinate to the central Committee.

Whoever violates these articles of discipline disrupts Party unity. Experience proves that some people violate Party discipline through not knowing what it is, while others, like Chang Kuo-tao, violate it knowingly and take advantage of many Party members' ignorance to achieve their treacherous purposes. Hence it is necessary to educate members in Party discipline so that the rank and file will not only observe discipline themselves, but will exercise supervision over the leaders so that they, too, observe it, thus preventing the recurrence of cases like Chang Kuo-tao's. If we are to ensure the development of inner-Party relations along the right lines, besides the four most important articles of discipline mentioned above we must work out a set of fairly detailed Party rules which will serve to unify the actions of the leading bodies at all levels.

PARTY DEMOCRACY

In the present great struggle, the Chinese Communist Party demands that all its leading bodies and all its members and cadres should give the fullest expression to their initiative, which alone can ensure victory. This initiative must be demonstrated concretely in the ability of the leading bodies, the cadres and the Party rank and file to work creatively, in their readiness to assume responsibility, in the exuberant vigor they show in their work, in their courage and ability to raise questions, voice opinions and criticize defects, and in the comradely supervision that is maintained over the leading bodies and the leading cadres. Otherwise, "initiative" will be an empty thing. But the exercise of such initiative depends on the spread of democracy in Party life. It cannot be brought into play if there is not enough democracy in Party life. Only in an atmosphere of democracy can large numbers of able people be brought forward. Ours is a country in which small-scale production and the patriarchal system prevail, and taking the country as a whole there is as yet no democratic life; consequently this state of affairs is reflected in our Party by insufficient democracy in Party life. This phenomenon hinders the entire party from exercising its initiative to the full. Similarly, it has led to insufficient democracy in the united front and in the mass movements. For these reasons, education in democracy must be carried on within the Party so that members can understand the meaning of democratic life, the meaning of the relationship between democracy and centralism, and the way in which democratic centralism should be put into practice. Only in this way can we really extend democracy within the Party and at the same time avoid ultra-democracy and the *laissez-faire* which destroys discipline.

It is also essential to extend democracy in our Party organizations in the army to the degree necessary to stimulate the initiative of the Party members and increase the combat effectiveness of the troops. However, there cannot be as much democracy in the Party organizations in the army as in the local Party organizations. Both in the army and in the local organizations, inner-Party democracy is meant to strengthen discipline and increase combat effectiveness, not to weaken them.

The extension of democracy in the Party should be seen as an essential step in its consolidation and development, and as an important weapon enabling it to be most active in the great struggle, to prove equal to its tasks, create fresh strength and surmount the difficulties of the war.

OUR PARTY HAS CONSOLIDATED ITSELF AND
GROWN STRONG THROUGH THE STRUGGLE ON TWO
FRONTS

Broadly speaking, in the last seventeen years our Party has learned to use the Marxist-Leninist weapon of ideological struggle against incorrect ideas within the Party on two fronts-- against Right opportunism and against "Left" opportunism.

Before the Fifth Plenary Session of the Sixth Central Committee, [2] our Party fought Chen Tu-hsiu's Right opportunism and Comrade Li Li-san's "Left" opportunism. It made great progress thanks to the victories achieved in these two inner-Party struggles. After the Fifth Plenary Session there were two further historic inner-Party struggles, namely, the struggles at the Tsunyi Meeting and in connection with the expulsion of Chang Kuo-tao.

The Tsunyi Meeting corrected serious errors of a "Left" opportunist character--errors of principle committed in the fight against the enemy's fifth "encirclement and suppression"

campaign--and united the Party and the Red Army; it enabled
the Central Committee of the Party and the main forces of the
Red Army to bring the Long March to a triumphant conclusion,
to advance to a forward position in the resistance to Japan and
to carry out the new policy of the Anti-Japanese National
United Front. By combating Chang Kuo-tao Right
opportunism, the Pasi and Yenan Meetings (the fight against
the Chang Kuo-tao line began at the Pasi Meeting [3] and
ended at the Yenan Meeting [4]) succeeded in bringing all the
Red forces together and in strengthening the unity of the whole
Party for the heroic struggle against Japan. Both kinds of
opportunist mistakes arose during the revolutionary civil war,
and their characteristic was that they were errors related to the
war.

What are the lessons which have been derived from these two
inner-Party struggles? They are:

(1) The tendency to "Left" impetuosity, which disregards both
the subjective and the objective factors, is extremely harmful to
a revolutionary war and, for that matter, to any revolutionary
movement--it was among the serious errors of principle which
were manifested in the struggle against the enemy's fifth
"encirclement and suppression" campaign, and which arose
from ignorance of the characteristics of China's revolutionary
war.

(2) The opportunism of Chang Kuo-tao, however, was Right
opportunism in the revolutionary war and was a combination of
a retreatist line, warlordism and anti-Party activity. It was only
with the overcoming of this brand of opportunism that large
numbers of cadres and Party members in the Fourth Front
Army of the Red Army, men of intrinsically fine quality and
with a long record of heroic struggle, were able to free

themselves from its toils and return to the correct line of the Central Committee.

(3) Striking results were achieved in the great organizational work of the ten years of the Agrarian Revolutionary War--in army building, government work, mass work and Party building. Had it not been for the support rendered by such organizational work to the heroic fighting at the front, we could not have kept up the bitter struggle against Chiang Kai-shek. However, in the latter part of that period serious errors of principle were made in the Party's policy concerning cadres and organization, errors which showed themselves in the tendency towards sectarianism, in punitiveness and in the policy of ideological struggle carried to excess. They were due both to our failure to eliminate the vestiges of the former Li Li-san line and to the political mistakes in matters of principle committed at the time. These errors, too, were corrected at the Tsunyi Meeting, and the Party was thus able to make the turn to a correct cadres policy and to correct organizational principles. As for Chang Kuo-tao's organizational line, it violated all Party principles, disrupted Party discipline and carried factional activity to the point of opposition to the Party, the Central Committee and the Communist International. The Central Committee did everything possible to overcome Chang Kuo-tao's iniquitous and erroneous line and to frustrate his anti-Party activity, and also tried to save Chang Kuo-tao himself. But as he stubbornly refused to correct his mistakes and resorted to double-dealing, and subsequently even betrayed the Party and threw himself into the arms of the Kuomintang, the Party had to take firm measures and expel him. This disciplinary action won the support not only of all Party members but of all people loyal to the cause of national liberation. The Communist International also endorsed the decision and denounced Chang Kuo-tao as a deserter and renegade.

These lessons, these achievements, have furnished us with the prerequisites for uniting the whole Party, for strengthening its ideological, political and organizational unity, and for successfully waging the War of Resistance. Our Party has consolidated itself and grown strong through the struggle on the two fronts.

THE PRESENT STRUGGLE ON TWO FRONTS

From now on, it is of paramount importance to wage a political struggle against Rightist pessimism in the War of Resistance, although it is still necessary to keep an eye on "Left" impetuosity. On questions of the united front and of Party and mass organization, we must continue the fight against the "Left" tendency towards closed-doorism if we are to achieve co-operation with the various other anti-Japanese parties and groups, expand the Communist Party and broaden the mass movement. At the same time, we must take care to combat the Right opportunist tendency towards co-operation and expansion which are unconditional in character, or otherwise they will both be hindered and be turned into capitulationist co-operation and unprincipled expansion.

Ideological struggle on the two fronts must suit the concrete circumstances of each case, and we must never approach a problem subjectively or permit the bad old habit of "sticking labels" on people to continue.

In the struggle against deviations, we must give serious attention to opposing double-faced behavior. As Chang Kuo-tao's career shows, the greatest danger of such behavior is that it may develop into factional activity. To comply in public but oppose in private, to say yes and mean no, to say nice things to a person's face but play tricks behind his back--these are all forms of double-dealing. Only by sharpening the vigilance of cadres and Party members against such behavior can we strengthen Party discipline.

STUDY

Generally speaking, all Communist Party members who can do so should study the theory of Marx, Engels, Lenin and Stalin, study our national history and study current movements and trends; moreover, they should help to educate members with less schooling. The cadres in particular should study these subjects carefully, while members of the Central Committee and senior cadres should give them even more attention. No political party can possibly lead a great revolutionary movement to victory unless it possesses revolutionary theory and a knowledge of history and has a profound grasp of the practical movement.

The theory of Marx, Engels, Lenin and Stalin is universally applicable. We should regard it not as a dogma, but as a guide to action. Studying it is not merely a matter of learning terms and phrases but of learning Marxism-Leninism as the science of revolution. It is not just a matter of understanding the general laws derived by Marx, Engels, Lenin and Stalin from their extensive study of real life and revolutionary experience, but of studying their standpoint and method in examining and solving problems. Our Party's mastery of Marxism-Leninism is now rather better than it used to be, but is still far from being extensive or deep. Ours is the task of leading a great nation of several hundred million in a great and unprecedented struggle. For us, therefore, the spreading and deepening of the study of Marxism-Leninism present a big problem demanding an early solution which is possible only through concentrated effort. Following on this plenary session of the Central Committee, I hope to see an all-Party emulation in study which will show who has really learned something, and who has learned more and learned better. So far as shouldering the main responsibility of leadership is concerned, our Party's fighting capacity will be much greater and our task of defeating Japanese imperialism will be more quickly accomplished if there are one or two hundred comrades with a grasp of Marxism-Leninism which is systematic and not fragmentary, genuine and not hollow.

Another of our tasks is to study our historical heritage and use the Marxist method to sum it up critically. Our national history goes back several thousand years and has its own characteristics and innumerable treasures. But in these matters we are mere schoolboys. Contemporary China has grown out of the China of the past; we are Marxist in our historical approach and must not lop off our history. We should sum up our history from Confucius to Sun Yat-sen and take over this valuable legacy. This is important for guiding the great movement of today. Being Marxists, Communists are internationalists, but we can put Marxism into practice only when it is integrated with the specific characteristics of our country and acquires a definite national form. The great strength of Marxism-Leninism lies precisely in its integration with the concrete revolutionary practice of all countries. For the Chinese Communist Party, it is a matter of learning to apply the theory of Marxism-Leninism to the specific circumstances of China. For the Chinese Communists who are part of the great Chinese nation, flesh of its flesh and blood of its blood, any talk about Marxism in isolation from China's characteristics is merely Marxism in the abstract, Marxism in a vacuum. Hence to apply Marxism concretely in China so that its every manifestation has an indubitably Chinese character, *i.e.,* to apply Marxism in the light of China's specific characteristics, becomes a problem which it is urgent for the whole Party to understand and solve. Foreign stereotypes must be abolished, there must be less singing of empty, abstract tunes, and dogmatism must be laid to rest, they must be replaced by the fresh, lively Chinese style and spirit which the common people of China love. To separate internationalist content from national form is the practice of those who do not understand the first thing about internationalism. We, on the contrary, must link the two closely. In this matter there are serious errors in our ranks which should be conscientiously overcome.

What are the characteristics of the present movement? What are its laws? How is it to be directed? These are all practical questions. To this day we do not yet understand everything about Japanese imperialism, or about China. The movement is developing, new things have yet to emerge, and they are emerging in an endless stream. To study this movement in its entirety and in its development is a great task claiming our constant attention. Whoever refuses to study these problems seriously and carefully is no Marxist.

Complacency is the enemy of study. We cannot really learn anything until we rid ourselves of complacency. Our attitude towards ourselves should be "to be insatiable in learning" and towards others "to be tireless in teaching".

UNITY AND VICTORY

Unity within the Chinese Communist Party is the fundamental prerequisite for uniting the whole nation to win the War of Resistance and build a new China. Seventeen years of tempering have taught the Chinese Communist Party many ways of attaining internal unity, and ours is now a much more seasoned Party. Thus we are able to form a powerful nucleus for the whole people in the struggle to win victory in the War of Resistance and to build a new China. Comrades, so long as we are united, we can certainly reach this goal.

NOTES

1. In his report to the 17th Congress of the C.P.S.U.(B.) in January 1934, Stalin said: ". . . after the correct political line has been laid down, organizational work decides everything, including the fate of the political line itself, its success or failure." (See *Problems of Leninism,* Eng. ed., FLPH, Moscow, 1954, p. 644.) He also dealt with the question of "proper selection of personnel". In his address in May 1935 delivered in the Kremlin Palace to the graduates from the Red Army Academies, Stalin put forward and explained the Hogan: "Cadres decide everything." *(Ibid.,* 661-62.) In his report to the 18th Congress of the C.P.S.U,(B) in March 1939, Stalin said: "After a correct political line has been worked out and tested in practice, the Party cadres become the decisive force in the leadership exercised by the Party and the state." (*Ibid.*, p. 784.)

2. The period referred to was that from the emergency meeting of the Political Bureau of the Fifth Central Committee of the Chinese Communist Party in August 1927 to the Fifth Plenary Session of the Sixth Central Committee in January 1934.

3. The Pasi Meeting was called by the Political Bureau of the Central Committee in August 1935 at Pasi, northwest of the county town of Sungpan, on the borders of northwestern Szechuan and southeastern Kansu. Chang Kuo-tao, leading a section of the Red Army, had broken away from the Central Committee, and was challenging its orders and attempting to undermine it. At this meeting the Central Committee decided to leave the danger zone for northern Shensi with those forces of the Red Army which obeyed its orders. However, Chang Kuo-tao led the Red Army units he had deceived southward to the area of Tienchuan, Lushan, the Big and Small Chinchuan and Ahpa, where he established a bogus central committee and came out publicly against the Party.

4. The Yenan Meeting was the enlarged meeting of the Political Bureau of the Central Committee of the Party held in Yenan in April 1937. Prior to this meeting large numbers of cadres and soldiers in the Red Army units under Chang Kuo-tao who had already become aware of his deception marched northward towards the Shensi-Kansu border area. On their way, however, some units acted on mistaken orders and switched westward to the area of Kanchow, Liangchow and Suchow, all in Kansu Province. Most of these were wiped out by the enemy and the rest made their way to Sinkiang and only later returned to the Shensi-Kansu border area. The other units had long since reached the Shensi-Kansu border area and joined forces with the Central Red Army. Chang Kuo-tao himself also turned up in northern Shensi and attended the Yenan Meeting. The meeting systematically and conclusively condemned his opportunism and rebellion against the Party. He feigned acquiescence but actually made preparations for his final betrayal of the Party.

COLLECTED WRITINGS
OF
CHAIRMAN MAO

POLITICS AND TACTICS

PART 5

THE ORIENTATION
OF
THE YOUTH MOVEMENT

Mao Zedong

Preface

May 4, 1939

This speech was delivered by Comrade Mao Zedong at a mass meeting of youth in Yenan to commemorate the twentieth anniversary of the May 4th Movement. It represented a development in his ideas on the question of the Chinese revolution.

Today is the twentieth anniversary of the May 4th Movement, and the youth of Yenan are all gathered here for this commemoration meeting. I shall therefore take the occasion to speak on some questions concerning the orientation of the youth movement in China.

First, May 4 has now been designated as China's Youth Day, [1] and rightly so. Twenty years have elapsed since the May 4th Movement, yet it is only this year that the day has been designated as the national Youth Day, and this is a most significant fact. For it indicates that the Chinese people's democratic revolution against imperialism and feudalism will soon reach a turning point. This revolution encountered repeated failures over several decades, but now there must be a change, a change towards victory and not another failure. The Chinese revolution is now going forward, forward to victory. The repeated failures of the past cannot and must not be allowed to recur, and they must be turned into victory. But has the change already taken place? No. It has not, nor have we yet won victory. But victory can be won. It is precisely in the present War of Resistance Against Japan that we are striving to reach the turning point from failure to victory. The May 4th Movement was directed against a government of national betrayal, a government which conspired with imperialism and sold out the interests of the nation, a government which oppressed the people. Was it not necessary to oppose such a government? If it was not, then the May 4th Movement was simply a mistake. It is obvious that such a government must be opposed, that a government of national betrayal must be overthrown. Just consider, long before the May 4th Movement Dr. Sun Yat-sen was already a rebel against the government of his day; he opposed and overthrew the Ching government. Was he right in doing so? In my opinion he was quite right. For the government he opposed did not resist imperialism but conspired with it, and was not a revolutionary government but one that suppressed the revolution. The May 4th Movement was a revolutionary movement precisely because it opposed a government of national betrayal. The youth of China should see the May 4th Movement in this light. Today, when the whole nation has militantly risen to resist Japan, we are determined to defeat Japanese imperialism, and we shall not tolerate any traitors or allow the revolution to fail again for we have taken warning from its failures in the past. With few exceptions, the whole youth of China is awakened and determined to win, and this is reflected in the designation of May 4th as Youth Day. We are advancing along the road to victory and, provided the whole people make a concerted effort, the Chinese revolution will definitely triumph through the War of Resistance.

Secondly, what is the Chinese revolution directed against? What are the targets of the revolution? As everybody knows, imperialism is one target and feudalism the other. What are the targets of the revolution at this moment? One is Japanese imperialism, and the other the Chinese collaborators. To make our revolution we must overthrow Japanese imperialism and the Chinese traitors. Who are the makers of the revolution? What is its main force? The common people of China. The motive forces of the revolution are the proletariat, the peasantry and all members of other classes who are willing to oppose imperialism and feudalism; these are the revolutionary forces opposing imperialism and feudalism. But who, among so many, are the basic force, the backbone of the revolution? The workers and the peasants, forming 90 per cent of the country's population. What is the nature of the Chinese revolution? What kind of revolution are we making today? Today we are making a bourgeois-democratic revolution, and nothing we do goes beyond its scope. By and large, we should not destroy the bourgeois system of private property for the present; what we want to destroy is imperialism and feudalism. This is what we mean by the bourgeois-democratic revolution. But its accomplishment is already beyond the capacity of the bourgeoisie and must depend on the efforts of the proletariat and the broad masses of the people. What is the goal of this revolution? To overthrow imperialism and feudalism and to establish a people's democratic republic. A people's democratic republic means a republic based on the revolutionary Three people's Principles. It will be different both from the semi-colonial and semi-feudal state of the present and from the socialist system of the future. Capitalists have no place in a socialist society, but they should still be allowed in a people's democracy. Will there always be a place for capitalists in China? No, definitely not in the future. This is true not only of China but of the whole world. In the future no country, whether it be Britain, the United States, France, Japan, Germany or Italy, will have any place for capitalists, and China will be no exception. The Soviet Union is a country which has already established socialism, and beyond all doubt the whole world will follow its example. China will certainly go over to socialism in the future; that is an irresistible law. But at the present stage our task is not to put socialism into practice, but to destroy imperialism and feudalism, change China's present semi-colonial and semi-feudal status, and establish people's democracy. This is what the youth of the whole country must strive for.

Thirdly, what are the lessons of the Chinese revolution? This question is also an important one for our youth to understand. Strictly speaking, China's bourgeois-democratic revolution against imperialism and feudalism was begun by Dr. Sun Yat-sen and has been going on for more than fifty years; as for foreign capitalist aggression against China, it has been going on for almost a hundred years. During that century, there was first the Opium War against British aggression, then came the War of the Taiping Heavenly Kingdom, then the Sino-Japanese

War of 1894, the Reform Movement of 1898, the Yi Ho Tuan
Movement, the Revolution of 1911, the May 4th Movement,
the Northern Expedition, and the war waged by the Red Army-
-although these struggles differed from each other, their
common purpose was to repel foreign enemies or change
existing conditions. However, it was only with Dr. Sun Yat-sen
that a more or less clearly defined bourgeois-democratic
revolution began. In the last fifty years the revolution started
by Dr. Sun Yat-sen has had both its successes and its failures.
Was not the Revolution of 1911 a success? Didn't it send the
emperor packing? Yet it was a failure in the sense that while it
sent the emperor packing, it left China under imperialist and
feudal oppression, so that the anti-imperialist and anti-feudal
revolutionary task remained unaccomplished. What was the
aim of the May 4th Movement? Its aim likewise was to
overthrow imperialism and feudalism, but it, too, failed, and
China still remained under the rule of imperialism and
feudalism. The same is true of the revolution known as the
Northern Expedition; it scored successes, but it too failed.
From the time the Kuomintang turned against the Communist
Party, [2] China again fell under the domination of imperialism
and feudalism. The inevitable result was the ten years' war
waged by the Red Army. But these ten years of struggle
fulfilled the revolutionary task only in parts of China and not in
the country as a whole. If we are to sum up the revolution
during the past decades we may say that it has won only
temporary and partial victories and not permanent and nation-
wide victory. As Dr. Sun Yat-sen said "The revolution is not
yet completed; all my comrades must struggle on." The
question now is: Why, after decades of struggle, has the
Chinese revolution not yet attained its goal? What are the
reasons? I think there are two: first, the enemy forces have
been too strong; second, our own forces have been too weak.
Because one side was strong and the other side weak, the
revolution did not succeed. In saying that the enemy forces

have been too strong, we mean that the forces of imperialism (the primary factor) and of feudalism have been too strong. In saying that our own forces have been too weak, we mean weak in the military, political, economic and cultural fields; but our weaknesses and our consequent failure to fulfill the anti-imperialist and anti-feudal task are chiefly due to the fact that the laboring people, the workers and peasants, constituting 90 per cent of the population, have not yet been mobilized. If we are to sum up the experience of the revolution of the past decades, we may say that the people throughout the country have not been fully mobilized and that the reactionaries have invariably opposed and sabotaged such mobilization. Only by mobilizing and organizing the workers and peasants, who comprise 90 per cent of the population, is it possible to overthrow imperialism and feudalism. Dr. Sun Yat-sen said in his Testament:

For forty years I have devoted myself to the cause of the national revolution with the aim of winning freedom and equality for China. My experiences during these forty years have firmly convinced me that to achieve this aim we must arouse the masses of the people and unite in a common struggle with those nations of the world which treat us as equals.

It is now more than ten years since Dr. Sun died, and if we add these on, the total is over fifty years. What is the lesson of the revolution during these years? Fundamentally, it is, "arouse the masses of the people". You should carefully study this lesson, and so should all China's youth. They must know that only by mobilizing the masses of workers and peasants, who form 90 per cent of the population, can we defeat imperialism and feudalism. Unless we mobilize the workers and peasants of the whole country, it will be impossible for us to defeat Japan and build a new China.

Fourthly, to return to the youth movement. On this very day twenty years ago there occurred in China the great historical event known as the May 4th Movement, in which the students participated; it was a movement of tremendous significance. What role have China's young people played since the May 4th Movement? In a way they have played a vanguard role--a fact recognized by everybody except the die-hards. What is a vanguard role? It means taking the lead and marching in the forefront of the revolutionary ranks. In the anti-imperialist and anti-feudal ranks of the Chinese people, there is a contingent composed of the country's young intellectuals and students. It is a contingent of considerable size and, even if the many who have given their lives are not included, it now numbers several million. It is an army on one of the fronts against imperialism and feudalism, and an important army too. But this army is not enough; we cannot defeat the enemy by relying on it alone, for when all is said and done it is not the main force. What then is the main force? The workers and peasants. Our young intellectuals and students must go among the workers and peasants, who make up 90 per cent of the population, and mobilize and organize them. Without this main force of workers and peasants, we cannot win the fight against imperialism and feudalism; we cannot win it by relying only on the contingent of young intellectuals and students. Therefore, the young intellectuals and students throughout the country must unite with the broad masses of workers and peasants and become one with them, and only then can a mighty force be created. A force of hundreds of millions of people! Only with this huge force can the enemy's strongholds be taken and his last fortresses smashed. In assessing the youth movement of the past from this viewpoint, we should call attention to a wrong tendency. In the youth movement of the last few decades, a section of the young people have been unwilling to unite with the workers and peasants and have opposed their movements; this is a counter-current in the youth movement. In fact, these people are not at all bright in their refusal to unite with the masses who make up 90 per cent of the population and in going so far as to oppose them outright. Is this a good tendency? I think not, because in opposing the workers and peasants they are in fact opposing the revolution; that is why we say it is a counter-current in the youth movement. A youth movement of that kind would come to no good. A few days ago I wrote a short article in which I noted:

In the final analysis, the dividing line between revolutionary intellectuals and non-revolutionary or counter-revolutionary intellectuals is whether or not they are willing to integrate themselves with the workers and peasants and actually do so.

Here I advanced a criterion which I regard as the only valid one. How should we judge whether a youth is a revolutionary? How can we tell? There can only be one criterion, namely, whether or not he is willing to integrate himself with the broad masses of workers and peasants and does so in practice. If he is willing to do so and actually does so, he is a revolutionary; otherwise he is a non-revolutionary or a counter-revolutionary. If today he integrates himself with the masses of workers and peasants, then today he is a revolutionary; if tomorrow he ceases to do so or turns round to oppress the common people, then he becomes a non-revolutionary or a counter-revolutionary. Some young people talk glibly about their belief in the Three People's Principles or in Marxism, but this does not prove anything. Doesn't Hitler profess belief in "socialism"? Twenty years ago even Mussolini was a "socialist"! And what does their "socialism" amount to? Fascism! Didn't Chen Tu-hsiu once "believe" in Marxism? What did he do later? He went over to the counter-revolution. Didn't Chang Kuo-tao "believe" in Marxism? Where is he now? He has run away and landed in the mire. Some people style themselves "followers of the Three People's Principles" or even old stalwarts of these Principles; but what have they done? It turns out that their Principle of Nationalism means conspiring with imperialism, that their Principle of Democracy means oppressing the common people, and that their Principle of People's Livelihood means sucking the people's blood. They affirm the Three People's Principles with their lips but deny them in their hearts. So when we assess a person and judge whether he is a true or false adherent of the Three People's Principles, whether he is a true or false Marxist, we need only find out how he stands in relation to the broad masses of workers and peasants, and then we shall know him for what he is. This is the only criterion, there is no other. I hope that the youth of our country will never allow themselves to be carried away by this sinister counter-current but will clearly recognize the workers and peasants as their friends and march forward to a bright future.

Fifthly, the present War of Resistance Against Japan marks a new stage--the greatest, most dynamic and most vigorous stage-- in the Chinese revolution. In this stage the youth shoulder tremendous responsibilities. Our revolutionary movement has gone through many stages of struggle in the last decades, but at no stage has it been so broad as in the present War of Resistance. When we maintain that the Chinese revolution now has features distinguishing it from the revolution in the past and that it will make the turn from failure to victory, we mean that the masses of the Chinese people have made progress, of which the progress of the youth is a clear proof. Hence the anti-Japanese war must and certainly will triumph. As everybody knows, the basic policy in this war is the Anti-Japanese National United Front, whose aim it is to overthrow Japanese imperialism and the Chinese collaborators, transform the old China into a new China, and liberate the whole nation from its semi-colonial and semi-feudal status. The present lack of unity in the Chinese youth movement is a serious weakness. You should continue to strive for unity, because unity is strength. You must help the youth of the whole country to understand the present situation, to achieve unity and to resist Japan to the end.

Sixthly and lastly, I want to speak about the youth movement in Yenan. It is the model for the youth movement throughout the country. The direction it is taking is in fact the orientation for the youth movement of the entire country. Why? Because it is the correct orientation. You see, in the matter of unity the youth of Yenan have acquitted themselves well, indeed very well. The youth of Yenan have achieved solidarity and unity. The young intellectuals and students, the young workers and peasants in Yenan are all united. Large numbers of revolutionary youth from all over the country, and even from Chinese communities abroad, have come to study in Yenan. Most of you attending this meeting today have come to Yenan from thousands of miles away; whether your surname is Chang or Li, whether you are a man or a woman, a worker or a peasant, you are all of one mind. Should this not be regarded as a model for the whole country? The youth in Yenan, besides being united among themselves, have integrated themselves with the masses of workers and peasants, and more than anything else this makes you a model for the whole country. What have you been doing? You have been learning the theory of revolution and studying the principles and methods for resisting Japan and saving the nation. You have been carrying out the campaign for production and have reclaimed thousands of *mou* of waste land. Confucius never reclaimed land or tilled the soil. When he ran his school, he had quite a number of students, "seventy worthies and three thousand disciples"-- quite a flourishing school! But he had far fewer students than there are in Yenan, and what is more, they would have disliked production campaigns. When a student asked him how to plough the fields, Confucius answered, "I don't know, I am not as good at that as a farmer." Confucius was next asked how to grow vegetables, and he answered, "I don't know, I am not as good at that as a vegetable gardener." In ancient times the youth of China who studied under a sage neither learned revolutionary theory nor took part in labor. Today, there is little revolutionary theory taught and there are no such things as production movements in the schools over vast regions of our country. It is only here in Yenan and in the anti-Japanese base areas behind the enemy lines that the young people are fundamentally different; they are really the vanguard in resisting Japan and saving the nation because their political orientation and their methods of work are correct. That is why I say the youth movement in Yenan is the model for the youth movement throughout the country. Our meeting today is highly significant. I have said all I wanted. I hope you will all study the lessons of the Chinese revolution in the last fifty years, develop its good points and discard its mistakes, so that the youth will be at one with the people of the whole country and the revolution will make the turn from failure to victory. When the youth and the whole nation are mobilized, organized and united, Japanese imperialism will be overthrown. Each young person must shoulder his responsibility. You must each be different from before and resolve to unite the youth and organize the people of the whole country for the overthrow of Japanese imperialism and the transformation of the old China into a new China. This is what I expect of all of you.

NOTES

1. May 4 was first adopted as China's Youth Day by the youth organization of the Shensi-Kansu-Ningsia Border Region. Under the pressure of the patriotic upsurge of the broad masses of young people, the Kuomintang government expressed its agreement. But it subsequently proclaimed March 29 as its own Youth Day (in Commemoration of the revolutionary martyrs who died during an uprising at Canton in 1911) because, fearing that the youth would turn revolutionary, it regarded the decision to observe May 4 as dangerous. However, May 4 continued to be observed as Youth Day in the revolutionary base areas under the leadership of the Communist Party, and was officially proclaimed China's Youth Day by the Administrative Council of the Central People's Government in December 1949 after the founding of the People's Republic of China.

2. "The Kuomintang turned against the Communist Party" here refers to the counter-revolutionary coups staged in 1927 by Chiang Kai-shek in Shanghai and Nanking and by Wang Ching-wei in Wuhan.

COLLECTED WRITINGS
OF
CHAIRMAN MAO

POLITICS AND TACTICS

PART 6

WIN THE MASSES

Preface

May, 1937

This was the concluding speech made by Comrade Mao Zedong at the National Conference of the Communist Party of China, held in May 1937.

The growing intensity of the revolutionary war makes it imperative for us to mobilize the masses in order to launch an immediate campaign on the economic front and undertake all possible and necessary tasks of economic construction. Why? Because all our present efforts should be directed towards gaining victory in the revolutionary war and, first and foremost, towards gaining complete victory in the fight to smash the enemy's fifth "encirclement and suppression" campaign [1] they should be directed towards securing the material conditions which will guarantee food and other supplies for the Red Army, towards bettering the life of the people and so stimulating their more active participation in the revolutionary war, towards organizing the masses on the economic front and educating them so as to provide fresh mass strength for the war, and towards consolidating the worker-peasant alliance and the democratic dictatorship of workers and peasants and strengthening proletarian leadership by building up the economy.

Such economic construction is essential for the attainment of all these objectives. This must be clearly understood by everyone engaged in revolutionary work. Some comrades have thought it impossible to spare time for economic construction because the revolutionary war keeps people busy enough, and they have condemned anyone arguing for it as a "Right deviationist". In their opinion economic construction is impossible in the midst of a revolutionary war and is possible only in the peaceful, tranquil conditions prevailing after final victory. Comrades, such views are wrong. Whoever holds them fails to realize that without building up the economy it is impossible to secure the material prerequisites for the revolutionary war, and the people will become exhausted in the course of a long war. Just consider! The enemy is enforcing an economic blockade, unscrupulous merchants and reactionaries are disrupting our finance and commerce, and the trade of our

Red areas with the outside is seriously hampered. Will not the revolutionary war be seriously affected unless these difficulties are overcome? Salt is very dear, and sometimes even unobtainable. Rice is cheap in the autumn and winter, but it becomes terribly dear in spring and summer. All this directly affects the life of the workers and peasants and prevents any improvement. And does it not affect our basic line--the alliance of workers and peasants? If the workers and peasants become dissatisfied with their living conditions, will it not affect the expansion of our Red Army and the mobilization of the masses for the revolutionary war? Therefore it is utterly wrong to think that no economic construction should be undertaken in the midst of the revolutionary war. Those who think this way often say that everything should be subordinated to the war effort, but they fail to understand that to dispense with economic construction would weaken the war effort rather than subordinate everything to it. Only by extending the work on the economic front and building the economy of the Red areas can we provide an adequate material basis for the revolutionary war, proceed smoothly with our military offensives and strike effective blows at the enemy's "encirclement and suppression" campaigns; only thus can we acquire the resources to enlarge the Red Army and push our front outwards to points thousands of *li* away, so that when the circumstances prove favorable, the Red Army will be able to attack Nanchang and Kiukiang free from all anxiety and, thus relieved of much of the task of provisioning itself, give its undivided attention to fighting; and only thus can we to a certain extent satisfy the material needs of the people so that they will join the Red Army or undertake other revolutionary tasks with even greater enthusiasm. Subordinating everything to the war effort means just this. Among those engaged in revolutionary work in various places, many do not yet understand the importance of economic construction in the revolutionary war, and there are many local governments which give little attention to discussing the problems of economic construction. The economic departments of the local governments are not yet well organized, and some are still without a director; in others some incompetent has been assigned simply to kill the post. The formation of co-operatives is still in the initial stage, and only in a few places has the work of regulating food supplies been started. There has been no propaganda among the people for the work of economic construction (though such propaganda is very important), and mass enthusiasm for it has not been aroused. All this is due to the failure to recognize the importance of economic construction. Through the discussions at this conference and through the reports you will make when you return to your posts, we must create mass enthusiasm for economic construction among all government personnel and among all workers and peasants. The importance of economic construction for the revolutionary war should be made clear to everyone, so that they will do their best to promote the sale of economic construction bonds, develop the co-operative movement, and set up public granaries and storehouses for famine relief everywhere. Each county must establish a sub-department for the regulation of food supplies, with branch offices in important districts and market centers. On the one hand, within our Red areas we should send grain from places with a surplus to those with a deficit, so that it will not pile up in one place and become unobtainable in another and its price will not be too low in one place and too high in another; on the other hand, we should send our grain surplus out of the Red areas in a planned way *(i.e.,* not in unlimited quantities) and bring in necessities from the White areas, thus avoiding exploitation by unscrupulous merchants. We must all do our best to develop agriculture and handicrafts and increase the output of farm implements and lime in order to ensure a bigger crop next year, and we must restore the output of such local products as wolfram, timber, camphor, paper, tobacco, linen, dried mushrooms and peppermint oil to former levels, and market them in the White areas in quantity.

Judged by volume, grain ranks first among the principal outgoing commodities in our trade with the outside areas. About three million piculs of unhusked rice are sent out yearly in exchange for necessary consumer goods, or an average of one picul a head of the three million population; it cannot, surely, be less than this. But who is handling this trade? It is handled entirely by the merchants who exploit us ruthlessly in the process. Last year they bought unhusked rice from the peasants in Wanan and Taiho Counties at fifty cents a picul and sold it in Kanchow for four yuan, making a sevenfold profit. Take another instance. Every year our three million people need about nine million yuan worth of salt and six million yuan worth of cotton cloth. Needless to say, this fifteen million yuan trade in salt and cloth has been entirely in the hands of the merchants; we have done nothing about it. The exploitation by the merchants is really enormous. For instance, they go to Meihsien and buy salt at one yuan for seven catties, and then sell it in our areas at one yuan for twelve ounces. Is this not shocking profiteering? We can no longer ignore such a state of affairs, and from now on we must handle this trade ourselves. Our department of trade with outside areas must make a great effort in this connection.

How shall we use the three million yuan from economic construction bonds? We plan to use it in the following way. One million will be allotted for the Red Army's war expenses, and two million will be loaned as capital to the co-operatives, the Bureau for the Regulation of Food Supplies and the Bureau of External Trade. Of the latter amount, the greater part will be used for expanding our external trade and the rest for expanding production. Our objective is not only to expand production but also to sell our products at fair prices to the

White areas and then purchase salt and cloth cheaply for distribution among our people, so as to break the enemy's blockade and check the merchants' exploitation. We must bring about the continued growth of the people's economy, greatly improve the livelihood of the masses and substantially increase our public revenue, thus laying firm material foundations for the revolutionary war and for economic construction.

This is a great task, a great class struggle. But we should ask ourselves, can it be accomplished in the midst of fierce fighting? I think it can. We are not talking about building a railway to Lungyen or, for the time being, even about building a motor road to Kanchow. We are not saying that there should be a complete monopoly of the sale of gram, or that the government should handle all the salt and cloth trade, valued at fifteen million yuan, to the total exclusion of the merchants. This is not the point we are making or what we are trying to do. What we are talking about and trying to do is to develop agriculture and the handicrafts, and send out grain and wolfram in exchange for salt and cloth, starting temporarily with a fund of two million yuan plus the money invested by the people. Is there anything here that we should not undertake, or that we cannot undertake and achieve? We have already started this work and achieved some results. This year's autumn harvest is between 20 and 25 per cent larger than last year's, or more than our original estimate of a 20 per cent increase. In the handicraft industries the production of farm implements and lime is being restored, and we are beginning to restore wolfram production. The output of tobacco, paper and timber is recovering. Much has been accomplished this year in the regulation of food supplies. A start has been made on importing salt. It is on these achievements that we base our firm belief in the possibility of further progress. Is it not clearly wrong to say that economic construction is impossible now and has to wait until the war is over?

It is thus clear that, at the present stage, economic construction must revolve around our central task, the revolutionary war. Today the revolutionary war is our central task, which economic construction should serve, centre on and be subordinated to. It would likewise be wrong to regard economic construction as the centre of all our present work to the neglect of the revolutionary war, or to conduct it apart from the revolutionary war. Not until the civil war is over will it be possible and necessary to regard economic construction as the centre of all our work. In the midst of a civil war, it is sheer delusion to try to carry out such peace-time economic construction as can and should be done in the future but not at present. The tasks for the present are those urgently demanded by the war. Every one of them should serve the war; none is a peace-time undertaking separate from the war. If any comrade entertains the idea of carrying out economic construction apart from the war, he should correct this mistake at once.

It will be impossible to get a rapid campaign going on the economic front without a correct style of leadership and correct methods of work. This, too, presents an important problem which this conference must solve. For the comrades here will have a great deal to do as soon as they return, and will have to give guidance to the many people who will be working with them. In particular, the comrades who are working at the township and city levels and in the co-operatives, the food departments, the trade departments and the purchasing offices, are personally engaged in the practical work of mobilizing the people to organize co-operatives, regulating and transporting food supplies, and managing our trade with the outside areas. If their style of leadership is wrong and if they do not employ correct and efficient methods, the work will be immediately affected, we shall fail to win mass support for the various tasks, and during the coming autumn and winter and next spring and summer we shall be unable to carry out the whole of the

Central Government's plan for economic construction. For these reasons I want to direct our comrades' attention to the following.

Firstly, mobilize the masses by various organizational means. In the first place, comrades on the presidiums and in the economic and finance departments of the government bodies at all levels must regularly put on their agenda and discuss, supervise and check up on such items of work as the sale of bonds, the formation of co-operatives, the regulation of food supplies and the promotion of production and trade. Next, the mass organizations, chiefly the trade unions and poor peasant leagues, must be moved into action. The trade unions should mobilize all their members to join these economic struggles. The poor peasant leagues are powerful bases for mobilizing the masses to build up co-operatives and subscribe to bonds, and they should be given vigorous leadership by district and township governments. Furthermore, we must conduct propaganda for economic construction at village or household meetings, explaining clearly how it is related to the revolutionary war and discussing in the most practical terms how to improve the livelihood of the masses and increase our strength for the struggle. We should appeal to the people to subscribe to bonds, develop co-operatives, regulate food supplies, consolidate finances and promote trade; we should call upon them to fight for these slogans and should heighten their enthusiasm. Our objectives cannot be attained unless we use various organizational means to mobilize the masses and conduct propaganda among them in the manner described, that is to say, unless the presidiums and the economic and finance departments of the government bodies at all levels actively attend to discussing and checking up on the work of economic construction, unless they spur the mass organizations into action and hold mass propaganda meetings.

Secondly, we must not be bureaucratic in our methods of mobilizing the masses. Bureaucratic leadership cannot be tolerated in economic construction any more than in any other branch of our revolutionary work. The ugly evil of bureaucracy, which no comrade likes, must be thrown into the cesspit. The methods which all comrades should prefer are those that appeal to the masses, *i.e.,* those which are welcomed by all workers and peasants. One manifestation of bureaucracy is slacking at work due to indifference or perfunctoriness. We must wage a stern struggle against this phenomenon. Commandism is another manifestation. To all appearances, persons given to commandism are not slackers; they give the impression of being hard workers. But in fact co-operatives set up by commandist methods will not succeed, and even if they appear to grow for a time, they cannot be consolidated. In the end the masses will lose faith in them, which will hamper their development. To push the sales of bonds in a commandist way and impose arbitrary quotas, regardless of whether people understand what the bonds are for and of how much they can afford, will ultimately arouse the people's displeasure and make it impossible to achieve good sales. We must reject commandism; what we need is energetic propaganda to convince the masses, and we should develop the co-operatives, promote the sales of bonds and do all the work of economic mobilization in accordance with the actual conditions and the real feelings of the masses.

Thirdly, large numbers of cadres are needed to extend the campaign of economic construction. This is not a matter of scores or hundreds of people, but of thousands and tens of thousands whom we must organize, train and send to the economic construction front. They will be the commanders and the broad masses the soldiers on the economic front. People often sigh over the shortage of cadres. Comrades, is there really a shortage? Innumerable cadres have come to the fore from among the masses who have been steeled in the agrarian struggles, the economic struggles and the revolutionary war. How can we say there is a shortage of cadres? Discard this mistaken view and you will see cadres all around you.

Fourthly, economic construction today is inseparable not only from the general task of the war but from other tasks as well. Only if there is a thorough check-up on land distribution [2] will it be possible to abolish feudal and semi-feudal ownership of land completely, enhance the peasants' enthusiasm for production and swiftly draw the peasant masses into economic construction. Only if the labor laws are resolutely enforced will it be possible to better the life of the workers, bring them speedily into active participation in economic construction and strengthen their leadership of the peasants. Only if there is correct leadership in the elections and in the exposure campaigns [3] which accompany the check-up on land distribution will it be possible to strengthen our government bodies so that they can give more vigorous leadership in the revolutionary war and in all our work, including economic work. The raising of the political and cultural level of the people through cultural and educational work is also a most important task in the development of the economy. That the expansion of the Red Army must not be neglected for a single day goes without saying. Everybody understands that without Red Army victories the economic blockade would be still tighter. On the other hand, economic growth and a better life for the masses will undoubtedly be of great help to the work of expanding the Red Army and inspiring the masses to march eagerly to the front. To sum up, if we achieve all the above tasks, including the very important new one of economic construction, and if we make them all serve the revolutionary war, then victory in the revolutionary war will undoubtedly be ours.

NOTES

1. Between 1930 and 1934 Chiang Kai-shek launched five large-scale onslaughts against the Red area centered on Juichin, Kiangsi; they were called "encirclement and suppression" campaigns. The fifth of such campaigns began in October 1 though Chiang Kai-shek had been making active preparations for it since the summer.

2. A campaign to check up land distribution was carried out in the Red area after the agrarian reform to ascertain whether the land had been properly redistributed.

3. Exposure campaigns were democratic campaigns in which the people were encouraged to expose misdeeds by the functionaries of the democratic government.